The cry among Christian leaders which involves bringing no less ¹ continues to grow louder. I was for *Transforming Your Nation* by my good friend Dexter Low. As I read it, I found many practical insights concerning implementation that could only come from a leader in the non-Western world. Dexter is a Malaysian, and this gives him a fresh perspective that we all need. This excellent book provides a significant step forward for all of us seeking to fulfill the Great Commission.

—Dr. C. Peter Wagner
Vice President, Global Spheres, Inc.

God's Mandate for Transforming Your Nation is a remarkable read. It is well-written and documented, and the reader will encounter the revelation on how they can fulfill God's purpose in the earth on both personal and corporate levels.

Many people today love to talk about God's will being done but have absolutely no grid on the "how to's" of seeing it accomplished.

Dexter Low has done us all a big favor through writing this book. Every believer needs to read it!

—Dr. Cindy Jacobs
Generals International
Dallas, Texas

Dexter Low has written a compelling book to help the body of Christ fulfill Jesus's Great Commission. *God's Mandate for Transforming Your Nation* documents strategies used in many cities and nations for transformation. Low also provides practical steps to help Christians engage in the process of changing their cities and their nations.

I highly recommend *God's Mandate for Transforming Your Nation* for anyone wanting to participate in bringing change to their sphere of influence.

—Dr. Barbara Wentroble
President, International Breakthrough Ministries
President, Breakthrough Business Leaders
Author of *Prophetic Intercession, Praying With Authority,*
Fighting for Your Prophetic Promises,
Empowered for Your Purpose,
Removing the Veil of Deception
Website: https://barbarawentroble.com

If there is one sin that greatly afflicts the church, it is the indifference of "Christians" to the deplorable condition of the world. Because as Christians, it is our calling to be God's hands and feet…to be His ambassadors.

This book brings every Christian closer to that calling, as it admonishes us to move from the spiritual to the practical, meaning, out of the four walls of the church and into the world—not to be like it, but to be its salt and light.

Congratulations to Dr. Dexter Low. You have painted a smile on the face of God in writing a much-needed book as this. God bless you in your future endeavors!

—Bishop Bro. Eduardo "Eddie" C. Villanueva
Spiritual Director and International President,
Jesus Is Lord Church Worldwide (JILCW)
Founder, Philippines for Jesus Movement (PJM)

Someone once said that a man with a theory is no match for a man with an experience. That makes a man with a theory and an experience the most valuable of all.

Dexter Low is such a man, and this book is the distilled wisdom of his diligent research and his noble life.

He is a student, a theologian, a practitioner, a statesman, an ambassador, a general; yet most of all he is one who identifies, commissions, encourages, equips, interconnects, and loves with the Father's love, sons and daughters called and willing to be the critical mass for the transformation of nations.

Dexter and his beloved Lily have been catalysts for such things in many cities including our soon-to-be-revealed jewel, Adelaide, South Australia.

—Mark Mudri
Member of Global Executive of Advocates International
Founder of Kingdom Facilitation Centre, Australia

I love *God's Mandate for Transforming Your Nation*! It's a great overall view of what our lives should be about—advancing God's kingdom in the earth. I think we will agree with Dr. Low that, "I believe nation transformation is the church's agenda of the future." Isaiah 9:7 says, "Of the increase of His government and peace there will be no end." I believe the kingdom came when King Jesus came, and it has been increasing ever since. Dr. Low gives wonderful, faith-building examples of transformation of society, and an action plan for nation transformation based on principles that have been shown to work. This book gave me great encouragement for the future that nation transformation can and will happen. I plan on giving a copy of this book to all our HAPN leaders around the world.

—Dr. John Benefiel
Presiding Apostle,
Heartland Apostolic Prayer Network (hapn.us)
Founder and Senior Pastor, Church on the Rock,
Oklahoma City (cotr.tv)

It has been my privilege and pleasure to have known Dexter Low for a number of years as a fellow pastor and colleague, when we were both serving in the National Evangelical Christian Fellowship of Malaysia.

Dexter has certainly expressed his burden to see the church go beyond its four walls to reach nations with the gospel and to be an effective influence in every sphere of society.

I commend him for his dedication and perseverance to publish this book, confirming his passion to see a more effective witness by the church to do her part to bring the kingdom of God to all levels of society.

May his efforts to produce this book be an encouragement to you!

—Rev. Dr. Prince Guneratnam
Senior Pastor, Calvary Church, Kuala Lumpur

God's Mandate for Transforming Your Nation, authored by my friend and colleague, Apostle Dexter Low, will take the body of Christ to a new level of revelation and application concerning the Dominion Mandate of Genesis 1:28.

No theory in this volume! Dexter presents examples from several nations of how cultural transformation is happening at this moment. His ministry, particularly in East Malaysia and the Philippines, is an inspiring story of nation transformation accompanied by the release of the supernatural power of God.

Dexter also gives us practical procedural guidelines on how church leaders, civil government leaders, and marketplace leaders work together as a team to lead the way for transformation to happen.

When you digest the truths in this book you cannot help but be encouraged that the Great Commission Jesus gave His church will be fulfilled in history and in the whole earth!

—Jim Hodges
President, Federation of Ministers and Churches International
Duncanville, Texas

This book has been in the making for over thirty years. My dear friend and brother in the Lord, Dr. Dexter Low, has been instrumental in nation transformation quietly, without fanfare, his entire life. The keys he shares in this book, I heard him speak prophetically in Malaysia, in Los Angeles, and in the Philippines, long before anyone heard of the Marketplace, Transformation of Nations, Spiritual War in the Heavenlies. He and his powerful spiritual partner, Dr. Lily Low, have raised up a nation of warriors who understand the battle plan and have labored unceasingly to change the hearts of the people, therefore changing the heart of the nation.

He is a spiritual giant, a general, an unsung hero to me, who is not without battle scars, but throughout his life, he and Dr. Lily have sacrificed to successfully pave the way for the next generation of leaders to come forth through their ministry at Vision Valley Center, a branch of Latter Rain Church and worldwide. Vision Valley Center is an indigenous church in Malaysia pioneered by Dr. Dexter and Dr. Lily Low. Dr. Dexter Low is a friend who is closer than a brother! He is a war general, not a peacetime general; a strategist who understands the battle.

"Touching Heaven" through intercessory and spiritual warfare prayer; "Changing Earth" through the dynamic power of the Holy Spirit is what Dr. Dexter and Dr. Lily Low have done for over thirty years.

Be blessed and encouraged as you read this book, knowing that it is not just words, but words that were inspired by the Holy Spirit to help us fulfill God's final command, "to make disciples of all nations, ethnic groups."

—Dr. Michael McKinney
President, Promise Christian University
Pasadena, California

Dexter Low's book is a must read for anyone hungry to learn where the twenty-first-century church needs to get to in the next ten to twenty years and beyond. Dexter brings a wealth of personal experience and reality anecdotes to illustrate his practical and insightful understanding of the Word of God. The front line of the gospel is continually moving westward in its journey to the ends of the earth—from Jerusalem around the globe and back to Jerusalem.

Today the front line of the gospel is moving through Asia and Oceania in the longitude band from China to Australia. There is a massive shift taking place away from Western Christianity with a fresh new Asian focus. The Western style of consumer Christianity is over. The day of celebrity Christianity has passed its use-by date. Asia is the future as it brings back authenticity won out of persecution and suffering. This geographic and spiritual movement re-engages with the call at the end of the Old Testament—as it brings forth fresh Asian emphasis to renew the God-given nuclear family...where the Fathers' hearts turns to the children and the children's hearts turn to the Father (see Malachi 4:6 and Luke 1:17).

This renewal reflects the highest spiritual priority of Jesus's relationship with His Daddy God, and God's oneness with His Son. This is the ultimate purpose in relationship that we are invited to in the gospel. In our day, when marriage and family are devolving in the West, there has never been a more important time to renew the true biblical identity of family as is happening with Christianity in Asia. Dexter serves us exceedingly well in articulating this massively needed shift in Christianity so needed both now and in the years ahead.

—Peter Kentley (Captain)
Executive Director, Christian Federation
www.christianfederation.net.au

Dexter Low shares key insights on how nations are transformed when aligned to God's purposes. As the family of believers in a nation covenant to walk together to please His heart, His commanded blessings overflow. The deeper our oneness in the spirit, the greater God's presence is manifested in our midst. This book is a treasure trove of encouragement and inspiration.

—Dr. Rev. David Demian
Director, Watchmen for the Nations
Pastoral Leadership Team, Church of Zion,
British Columbia, Canada

Most of us know of the truth of the last book in the Old Testament that the Lord is sending Elijah to restore the hearts of the father to sons and sons to fathers (Mal. 4:5–6); few really realize that unless there is a real heart turning between the two generations, a curse of biblical magnitude is really coming on every nation.

Also, the Apostle Paul revealed an ancient mystery that God has an *intent* for the church to demonstrate *His* wisdom and power to the ruling principalities and powers (Eph. 3:9–10) so as to set the nations free to release the greatest harvest.

As history unfolds during this time in the kingdom of God, *God's Mandate for Transforming Your Nation* is a "must read" for all pastors and leaders. In our time we live in a global world where we can be any place within hours, or even communicate electronically with anyone, anywhere, within a matter of minutes. It is critical for pastors and leaders to understand the principles and seize the opportunities available to advance the kingdom of God. Dexter Low has spent his lifetime pouring his heart into the harvest field. His book is a treasure chest of wisdom for pastors and leaders, but more than anything, he knows and walks in the value of spiritual fathers in the raising up of the next generation. I have known Dexter Low personally for many years, and he is one of the original fathers in Malaysia of the Family Journey, which is pivotal to the ongoing global family journey.

—GIDEON CHIU
CHURCH OF ZION

In this book Dexter details his personal journey from the traditional mindset of "doing church" to a kingdom mind-set of fathering ministries and transforming nations.

He rightly calls for the church to be more than just a fishing boat, but a battleship; to recognize the seven mountains of culture and to impact the world beyond the four walls of the church.

He also provides a helpful overview of the various movements God is working through in our day to bring about reconciliation, empowerment, and transformation. As you read this book, you will be inspired to make changes in the way you "do church" and to follow in his footsteps.

—REV. DR. NAOMI DOWDY, SINGAPORE
FORMER SENIOR PASTOR, TRINITY CHRISTIAN CENTRE
FOUNDER, CHANCELLOR, TCA COLLEGE
FOUNDER, NAOMI DOWDY MINISTRIES

GOD'S MANDATE

★ ★ ★ *For* ★ ★ ★

TRANSFORMING YOUR
NATION

DEXTER LOW

CREATION
HOUSE

God's Mandate for Transforming Your Nation by Dexter Low
Published by Creation House
A Charisma Media Company
600 Rinehart Road
Lake Mary, Florida 32746
www.charismamedia.com

Unless otherwise noted, all Scripture quotations are from the New King James Version of the Bible. Copyright © 1979, 1980, 1982 by Thomas Nelson, Inc., publishers. Used by permission.

Scripture quotations marked KJV are from the King James Version of the Bible.

Scripture quotations marked NAS are from the New American Standard Bible. Copyright © 1960, 1962, 1963, 1968, 1971, 1972, 1973, 1975, 1977, 1995 by the Lockman Foundation. Used by permission. (www.Lockman.org)

Scripture quotations marked NIV are taken from the Holy Bible, New International Version®, NIV®. Copyright © 1973, 1978, 1984, 2011 by Biblica, Inc.™ Used by permission of Zondervan. All rights reserved worldwide. www.zondervan.com The "NIV" and "New International Version" are trademarks registered in the United States Patent and Trademark Office by Biblica, Inc.™

Design Director: Justin Evans
Cover design by Justin Evans

Visit the author's website: www.dexterlow.com.

Library of Congress Cataloging-in-Publication Data: 2016930251
International Standard Book Number: 978-1-62998-519-0
E-book International Standard Book Number: 978-1-62998-520-6

While the author has made every effort to provide accurate telephone numbers and Internet addresses at the time of publication, neither the publisher nor the author assumes any responsibility for errors or for changes that occur after publication.

First edition

16 17 18 19 20 — 9 8 7 6 5 4 3 2 1
Printed in Canada

Firstly, I dedicate this book to my family who has stood by me over the years both in my ministry and in my journey in writing my book: my beloved wife, Lily Low; my children—Elijah and Sarah Low, and their children, Madison and Aiden; Debbie and Caleb Tan, with their children, Caylie, Dylan, and Dayson; Ebbie and Joey Chiang, with their children, Ryan, Noel, Ethan, and Ian Asher; Victory and Bernice Low; and Anna Grace and Elisha Swee, with their child, Eleora.

Secondly, I would love to dedicate this book to pastors, leaders, and members in my church network, The Latter Rain Church, that are both in Malaysia and in other nations. They have been a source of joy and inspiration to my life. Their loyalty, love, and faithfulness to me have no bounds; for that I shall always be grateful.

Lastly, excellent servants of God whom God used to touch and impact my life over the years: C. Peter Wagner, Cindy Jacobs, Barbara Wentroble, Jim Hodges, Chuck Pierce, Mike and Adelle McKinney; and over the last few years, John Benefiel, Gideon Chiu, and David Demian.

ACKNOWLEDGMENTS

$\mathcal{I}$ AM DEEPLY GRATEFUL to Cindy Jacobs and Barbara Wentroble for giving me specific, prophetic words to write a book. Dr. C. Peter Wagner, my mentor from Fuller Theological Seminary, has been instrumental in giving me three pieces of crucial advice after reading the first draft of my manuscripts more than ten years ago, in 2005, including getting a US editor and approaching Charisma Media (Creation House) to publish my book.

A chance meeting with Steve Strang at Global Spheres inaugural conference, followed by breakfast with him, was divinely arranged—from total rejection in regard to publishing my book (as I was a non-US citizen, and therefore they could not sell my book), to now extending a contract for my book to be published by Creation House.

Right from the start, I was grateful to my wife, Lily Low, and my children, especially Elijah Low and Ebbie Low, for showing great interest and offering all kinds of help to get me started. Jeremiah Tan was gracious to collate all my materials, as was Christina Ong for offering her services to be my local editor.

My close friends Drs. Mike and Adelle McKinney, Hank Rooney, and Diwa Guinigundo (Deputy Governor of Philippines Central Bank) continued to encourage me to write and complete my book over the years and were a source of strength and encouragement.

Barbara Wentroble was very kind to introduce her editor, Norma Gorter, to assist me as US editor. Norma's work was invaluable, and her suggestions and advice made a big difference. My book evolved from a thesis-like approach to a book that is easy to read with exciting, factual testimonies. Norma's unrelenting push for my book to end on the high note caused me to delay finishing my book, but it was worthwhile. The high note demonstrated that the Lord allowed me to see the fruit of the ministry. The ministry that took place over several years is cutting-edge and risky, but the voice of the Lord gave direction, and we did not shrink back from the revelation for the new generations. As pioneers, we had our challenges, but God proved that He is faithful when we follow His strategies.

My gratitude to Allen Quain and the Charisma Media/Creation House team for their help and excellent work as they provided their support and encouragement regarding my manuscript.

Most of all, my gratitude to the Lord Jesus Christ, my chief inspiration, Savior, and King, for saving my life and calling me to serve Him globally.

Blessings,
Dexter Low

TABLE *of* CONTENTS

FOREWORD

*T*HERE IS A great likelihood that many Christians today feel they have maximized their delivery of the Great Commission based on the number of souls they have led to the knowledge and acceptance of the Lord Jesus Christ, discipled and taught. Indeed Christians have this theological and biblical construct which they have inherited from well-meaning Christian leaders, living the gospel within the safe environment of their sanctuaries and families. There is a feeling of great comfort and even relief that our Christian responsibility begins with evangelism and ends with discipleship. Is this what Jesus had in mind when the Holy Spirit was released to His people, when we were mandated to occupy until He comes, when He declared that God's will shall be done on earth as it is in heaven, that the government is upon His shoulders?

This is the sad state of the church until we begin to hear about kingdom dominion, standing in the gap for the nation; healing of the nations; destinies of nations; the various calls of God to covenant, restoration, holiness, harvest; the redemptive call; God's move of the church from fellowship to a large, effective force on the earth!

Dutch Sheets and Chuck Pierce's mission to the fifty states of the United States (2005) is just as powerful as their profession that "God is riding across this nation once again, lighting fires of cleansing and revival." God indeed wants the nations of the world to partner with Him in establishing the kingdom of God on earth. Once again in 2015 and 2016, Sheets and Pierce are on a mandate from God to pursue an Awakening Movement across the fifty states.

Dr. Peter Wagner's book *Dominion! How Kingdom Action Can Change the World* (2008) further drives home the point that the urgent mandate of God for the church is to "actively engage in transforming society." His message is very compelling: "It should be obvious to anyone that for society as a whole to change, each one of these molders of culture (religion, family, government, arts and entertainment, media, business and education) have powerful need to be led or 'dominated' by persons of goodwill, whether Christians or non-Christians." Domination, in this context, is commanding global influence for the betterment of mankind.

More and more Christian apostles and prophets are getting their "feet wet" in the more difficult task of the church, and this is to engage the real world in establishing God's dominion over the affairs of mankind even in media, business, and education. For many years now, focus has migrated from church evangelism and growth as well as discipleship and intimacy with God to using all these facets of church activities and fulfilling the Great Commission to help change the destinies and purposes of nations. God speaks and releases the anointing on both peoples and nations.

This is the meaningful, historical context of Brother Dexter Low's book, *God's Mandate for Transforming Your Nation*. This book chronicles episodes and emerging trends of the church spearheading the cause of national and social transformation in various jurisdictions and territories including his own country, Malaysia; my country, the Philippines; and nations in other regions of the world.

Brother Dexter is right on the spot in saying that "God's mandate is to restore all people and all nations to their original intent by fulfilling the Great Commission."

I can confirm many of Brother Dexter's grip and commitment to nation transformation and his very incisive observations. Brother Dexter and his wife, Sister Lily, led us in our intimate walk with God starting in the late 1990s. He mentored us, taught us, and loved us as they held our hands in breaking through the traditional boundaries of the church. On our return from a two-year stint at the International Monetary Fund in 2003, he ordained me as senior pastor of the Fullness of Christ International Ministry, which we founded with other elders in 1986. He explained and challenged me to take up the cause of nation transformation. For the next two years while serving as an officer of the Bangko Sentral ng Pilipinas, I buried myself in the study of nation and social transformation, covering case studies of what it would take for a number of cities to take dominion and install the rulership of Jesus Christ in almost all human activities and pillars of society.

In September 2005, we were emboldened by the move of God in the Philippines and organized the first Touching Heaven, Changing Earth Apostolic and Prophetic Conference. With other church leaders in the US, Malaysia, and the Philippines, declarations were released about God's ruling and reigning in the Philippines and prophesied that the Philippines would start pursuing its destiny as a nation of God. Brother Dexter spoke passionately during the Conference on destinies of nations. More than ten years and thirty city and provincial conferences later, during which the body of Christ has sustained its intercession for the Philippines, the nation has moved very quickly from once the economic laggard in Asia to an emerging tiger, a bright star in a dark region of nations. More and more Christians have moved to various positions of leadership in government, business and economy, media, arts and entertainment, education, and culture including family life. Starting December 2010, Psalm 33:12 has been emblazoned on the nation's new generation banknotes in all denominations, allowing God's rule to extend even in the economy and business throughout the Philippines. The Philippine peso has become one of the most stable currencies in Asia and the Pacific, both in nominal and real terms. Over 100 million people in their daily lives have been blessed reading God's assurance being impressed upon their minds and in their hearts: "Blessed is the nation whose God is the Lord, the people he chose for his inheritance" (see Psalm 33:12).

We are planning regional and national congresses of like-minded Christian leaders shortly with the aim of establishing the church as a social force in shaping a righteous and honest government; a resilient and robust economy and business community; relevant and godly educational system; and responsible media, entertainment, and culture. Today in the Philippines good governance is now a buzzword, but it is more than a fashionable phrase. Institution building is now a must.

Brother Dexter's work will definitely be a must in this endeavor. After much concentrated study and practical experience, he has formalized all his propositions for nation transformation. Church leaders in the Philippines and elsewhere will definitely find this book indispensable, giving us in no uncertain terms a glimpse of God's true mandate and plan for His church and the nations. Brother Dexter has always been passionate about God's cause of healing and transforming the nations, offering concrete strategies to shepherd the process. I pray that those who will read and learn from this book will also catch Brother Dexter's contagious argument that churches should be engaged in business so that money would be available in advancing the cause of the kingdom. As Dr. Wagner rightly pointed out, transforming society costs money. That should convince everyone that only when the church takes dominion can social change and nation transformation begin to happen including the transference of wealth from the ungodly to the people of God.

To God be the glory!

—BROTHER DIWA C. GUINIGUNDO
FULLNESS OF CHRIST INTERNATIONAL MINISTRIES
MANDALUYONG CITY, METRO MANILA
PHILIPPINES

INTRODUCTION
GOD'S MANDATE *for*
TRANSFORMING YOUR NATION

$\mathcal{W}$HAT IS GOD's mandate for transforming your nation? *You might ask that question.*

Yes, I have discovered God's mandate for transforming your nation and mine. This is not a vision that will never materialize or a theory that never becomes a reality. God's mandate is to restore all people and all nations to their original intent by fulfilling the Great Commission.

For many years I believed that as Christians, nations should be discipled according to the Great Commission. "Jesus came to them and said, 'All authority in heaven and on earth has been given to me. Therefore go and make disciples of all nations'" (Matt. 28:18–19, NIV). Although I wanted to find more information, I wasn't able to find books or others who discussed these scriptures. Almost everything that I found was about evangelization and bringing souls into salvation, but that didn't satisfy my desire for making disciples.

Before attending Fuller Theological Seminary, church planting was my emphasis. When I started attending Fuller, I focused on church growth. I completed my master's degree; however, C. Peter Wagner, who was mentoring me, left Fuller Seminary before I could complete the doctorate program. During this time, I had not only read about others but also met others who were having great success with church growth concepts while building their ministries. I put every effort into following that pattern of ministry. But alas, it didn't seem to turn out the way I had planned.

Then a few years ago I started to hear the words, "nation transformation." Immediately, my spirit was inspired. Then, during a season of ministry in the Philippines, I began to see results that satisfied my deepest desires for fulfilling my vision for building the kingdom of God.

Two of my very close friends—Eddie Villanueva, founder and bishop of the Jesus Is Lord (JIL) Church in the Philippines; and Diwa Guinigundo, now Deputy Governor of the Central Bank—shared with me about their burden for their nation. They said that the Philippines was second only to

Japan in terms of growth and development. On January 3, 1949, the Central Bank of the Philippines (now the Bangko Sentral ng Pilipinas) was created, including the vested power from administering the banking and credit system of the country. Over the years, the country has deteriorated due to corruption and ungodliness that infiltrated the nation. During the strong economic years, one Philippine peso was robust and equivalent to one US dollar, but nowadays it is more like forty-seven pesos to one USD.

As I started to focus my vision on how this nation could be changed, my heart felt compelled to join with my Filipino friends to see the nation transformed. We gathered pastors together, meeting in both large and small groups.

In 2005 the first conference for nation transformation was held in the prestigious Philippine International Convention Center (PICC) with the theme "Touching Heaven, Changing Earth." A second conference organized by the Central Bank Christian Fellowship was held March 2–3, 2007. We expected an attendance of five hundred pastors, but one thousand pastors attended. This conference was a most significant event because it prepared the Republic of the Philippines for the approaching elections and a time to mobilize great shifts in political leadership. Diligently we prayed for those who were godly and ethically sound to be elected.

During our first convention in May 2005, the Philippine peso was traded at fifty-six pesos to one US dollar. As of May 2007, it was nearly forty-eight pesos to one USD; and now it is about forty-seven pesos to one USD. Why this improvement? Because of one government agency, the Central Bank. It has had an A rating for several years and is considered a bright spot in Southeast Asia. Godly men and women within were rising up to do something great for the nation. Moody's raised the Philippines's sovereign rating to Baa2 from Baa3 and said the outlook was stable. Bangko Sentral ng Pilipinas kept the rate it pays lenders for overnight deposits at 4 percent,[1] as predicted by all eighteen economists in a Bloomberg News survey.[1] In 2015 the Philippines was ranked thirteenth out of forty-two countries in the Asia-Pacific region, with an overall score above the world and regional averages.[2]

I began to be involved with nation transformation and to study together with those who are involved such as Wagner, whom I had worked with in the spiritual warfare network. I started developing relationships with Cindy Jacobs and George Otis Jr. His findings about societal transformation were capsulated in the Transformations video documentary series. In the first series he investigated four cities that had been transformed, and the authentic testimonies helped us to see that transformation is not just a theory but can be a reality. The documentaries focused on enabling communities to discover the pathway to genuine revival and societal transformation.

According to George Otis Jr., one of the principal elements for transformation is "persevering leadership." For me, it was not only leadership but alignments; aligning with others who are like-minded to form alliances to fulfill the mission of transformation.

I was challenged to see that the Philippines fulfills her destiny as the first Christian nation in Asia, one befitting to be a model for other nations to follow. A nation whose God is the Lord, espousing kingdom values such as righteousness, justice, and good governance; a nation blessed by God to be economically prosperous, successful in eradication of poverty and corruption. I have a great desire to see the Philippines take her rightful place as a leader among many Asian nations and a beacon of hope to many nations.

Leadership is needed in nation transformation. Could it be possible that over the last ten years or so, the church had gone on the wrong track in trying to see cities being transformed? We thought that when church leaders came together to pray over cities, the cities would be transformed. But that was not *it*.

Gradually, most people started to realize that nation transformation will take place when we touch and change the seven primary pillars of society: Family, Religion, Government, Education, Business, Arts and Entertainment, and Media. These seven pillars are like seven primary spheres of influence in culture. God's intended purposes need to be established over all these spheres in order to be in strategic places of influence in culture and position to change policies. We can be the keys to begin realigning all that they are doing in these areas and transform the culture to kingdom principles. Working independently, church leaders are not able to reach all of society. It is evident that marketplace leaders are the ones who can effectively change and influence the nation's society. Aligning with the right people and groups produces a synergy that is able to cause transformation.

I believe nation transformation is the church's agenda of the future. Much of the worldwide Christian agenda ended by the year 2000, including the AD2000 and Beyond Movement. Many were hoping Christ would come by the year 2000. But it didn't happen then and is not happening now.

The question we are now asking is this: *What is the church's mission for the future?*

Do we have any good, solid, long-term plan? The late Bill Bright came up with some insights on that. Founded in 2002, the Global Pastors Network (GPN) has a goal to bring leaders around the world together to fulfill the Great Commission by the year 2021. This was to be accomplished by winning one billion souls and planting five million churches. However, I do not see any action at this time, and I do not believe this agenda will work because it is based on the same traditional approach based upon church planting and evangelism. On the other hand, nation transformation will be the direction of the future. This will navigate the focus of missions and theology, especially those that practice kingdom theology or "dominion theology."

The Great Commission is to teach the nations to follow the commands of Jesus:

> Therefore go and make disciples of all nations, baptizing them in the name of the Father and of the Son and of the Holy Spirit, and teaching them to obey everything I have commanded you. And surely I am with you always, to the very end of the age.
>
> —MATTHEW 28:19–20, NIV

The time is now. More than ever, it is crucial for the church to finally take up the challenge to raise up and equip men and women with a fervent desire to act as agents of nation transformation for this fallen world. God is moving fast in these times—but is the church keeping up with Him?

CHAPTER 1
MAKE DISCIPLES *of* ALL NATIONS

Go therefore and make disciples of all the nations, baptizing
them in the name of the Father and the Son and the Holy
Spirit, teaching them to observe all that I commanded you.
—MATTHEW 28:19–20, NAS

*J*ESUS MANDATED THE Great Commission to us, the church. Basically, this mandate gave His disciples the authority for transformation of all the nations.

What does the word *nation* mean?

Donald McGavran, founder of Church Growth, was the first to introduce the concept of "nation." Later, Dr. Ralph D. Winter, founder of the US Center for World Mission, expounded on the concept of the Great Commission: *make disciples of all nations.* He said the word *nations* comes from the Hebrew word *ethne*. Ethne is not just geographical or political but also refers to people groups.[1] Since then, missiologists have been focusing on reaching out to the unreached people groups as part of their responsibility in fulfilling the Great Commission. For example, Malaysia is one nation, but within that one nation are many people groups, including the numerous tribes in East Malaysia.

However, we may need to change our thinking and mind-set regarding the phrase "make disciples of all nations." Common interpretation of *discipling the nations* has been to evangelize the individuals of the nations. However, God has called us to disciple the *nations.* This means to bring into alignment all the various aspects of ethne or nation in line with God's purposes. We must not have the narrow mind-set that the Great Commission is just about winning souls for the Lord. By doing so, we have already divorced ourselves from being involved in many other aspects of nation building.

In 1974 John Stott, a British Christian and one of the principal authors of the Lausanne Covenant, spoke at the World Congress on Evangelism, also known as the Lausanne I conference. He spoke about the social aspect of evangelical involvement, known as social action, which is to help the poor, orphans, widows, and the handicapped. Evangelicals then started to place the cultural mandate alongside the evangelistic mandate.

Both John Stott and Dr. Ralph Winters played important roles in helping the church to understand the Great Commission, but currently the Holy Spirit is revealing more things to the church. Discipling the nations is not just about evangelizing, but it also means to change the various systems of a nation, which I prefer to term as the primary influences of nation transformation, a concept popularized by Dr. C. Peter Wagner in his book *The Church in the Workplace.*[2]

Let us take a closer look at how nation transformation can possibly work at three basic levels:

+ Level 1: Community Level
+ Level 2: City Level
+ Level 3: National Level

LEVEL 1—COMMUNITY TRANSFORMATION: THE SELAKO PEOPLE

The ministry of the Holy Spirit among the Selako people is an example of community transformation. The Selako people group located in East Malaysia is one of the smaller tribes in the world, with a current population of about 19,000, living at the southern tip of West Borneo, known as the state of Sarawak. A branch of Dayak people from Borneo Island, they have been very resistant to the gospel for the last fifty years or so and even hostile toward missionary efforts, greeting mission teams with brandished knives. The Latter Rain Church started ministry in their midst in the 1980s, through students studying under committed Christian teachers in the city of Kuching, the capital of East Malaysia. Through these Selako students, revival broke out amongst the people, and it spread to the villages of Sebako, Pueh and Biawak.

Education

The role of teachers cannot be underestimated. Over time they have made a powerful social and spiritual impact upon the lives of students. In Latter

Rain and many other churches, the teachers are dedicated to the academic well-being of their students and work hard at grooming them for better study achievement. Through these churches, many graduates who became professionals are being raised into new levels of leadership. Quite a number of young people have succeeded in education and now hold good positions in various cities of the nation. In a sense, a war is waging against poverty, illiteracy, and unemployment, gradually redeeming success for God's people.

Latter Rain Church has many such dedicated teachers in the cities and villages throughout Sarawak such as Miri, Podam and Sri Aman. Now, even local natives are pursing the teaching profession.

Recently at a school in Sri Aman, the heartland of the Iban tribe, a principal who is of the Muslim faith commented during the weekly assembly that students who want to do well should go to Latter Rain Church. They had begun associating success in studies with the positive influence the church has on students!

Leadership influence

In these villages the gospel has come with signs, wonders, and miracles. During the first healing campaign, a dying 105-year-old man was healed, and he walked back to his home to live for three more years! Later, this same man gave two pieces of land for the church building and a cemetery. Power encounters with a witch doctor, belief in spirits and demons, and spiritual warfare were experienced. In Pueh, people associated strong winds with angry spirits and were influenced heavily by a *bomoh* (witch doctor). The bomoh became very angry with Christians. As one of the bomoh watched a deliverance, the bomoh saw many spirits coming out, and he himself was struck unconscious. When Christians went there to evangelize, a great spiritual deliverance occurred. People freely gave their charms to be burned. The people believe their charms have magical power.

Our purpose was to not only see them receive salvation but also to see a transformation of their lives and community. When the head man of Sebako became a Christian, he used his influence and steered the community toward many positive changes.

Indigenization

When the local people from various tribes have become Christians, we helped to build churches and introduced music and songs in their own languages. It is important to maintain their original culture and heritage, but we were able to bring biblical perspectives into their cultural elements such as dance, the practice of circumcision, language, and even rites of passage such as weddings and funerals. Some cultural elements unique to the people are not put aside. Instead, they remain relevant and are redeemed for the Lord.

Engagement with government

Prior to the Latter Rain Church ministry among the Selako people, their villages did not have proper roads or electricity. We felt a strong urgency that the church needed to be engaged with the government and to be partners with the government in nation building. This covers various areas including infrastructure, agriculture, and supporting the right political leaders. Therefore, we encouraged them to work closely with the former state assemblyman and the former Assistant Minister of Agriculture to bring development to the villages.

Since then, the villages actively have become very much more developed, with good roads, electricity, and other amenities. The people reap the benefits of godly leaders.

Business

Pastor Daron Tan, pastor of Trinity Community Centre, Kuching, in Sarawak, Malaysia, is founder and managing director of Borneo Echo Streams (BES), an enterprise that specializes in catching and exporting ornamental fish. Started several years ago, BES not only provides for Tan's family but also gives sustainable employment for poor villages. "BES encourages full-time ministers in the third world to develop sustainable means of impacting their field through work and ministry."[3] According to Daron Tan, business and ministry can be complementary for "a pastor working in a poor community [who] will be a burden to his congregation if he expects them to support him. If he depends on external financial support to keep his ministry afloat, he may have to stop serving when this aid is not forthcoming for various reasons."[4]

Daron is also chairman of Kuching Ministers' Fellowship. This economic model is important to encourage the youth to stay in the village instead of joining the thousands to migrate to towns and cities to look for work. "A few villages in southern Sarawak and Kalimantan Barat have already acquired sufficient skills to work with BES in developing large-scale ornamental fish breeding programmes."[5]

LEVEL 2—CITY TRANSFORMATION: ALMOLONGA, GUATEMALA

Almolonga, Guatemala is a phenomenal example of city transformation. In 1980, I was in Almolonga together with Dr. C. Peter Wagner and Cindy Jacobs for the World Congress of Evangelism event hosted by Harold Caballeros of El Shaddai Church in Guatemala.

Almolonga appears to experience great blessings from God with very tangible forms! I can personally testify that in Almolonga, a carrot grows as big as an arm! While at the airport waiting to depart back to the States, we saw one carrot that was big enough to be shared among the group of twenty. The cabbages were *five times* the size of a normal cabbage! Here is how Wagner describes the transformation that has taken place in that city:

> Twice I have visited Almolonga, Guatemala, a city of about 20,000 indigenous people, located deep in the Guatemalan highlands. What I saw was a true faith builder for city transformation.
>
> The process began in the mid-1970s when Mariano Riscajche, a struggling pastor, began casting out demons, especially the demon of alcoholism. Since then, transformation has come in several areas:
>
> *Spiritual awakening.* The percentage of born-again Christians in Almolonga has risen dramatically from less than 5 percent to 90 percent at the present time. Previously the city was under a dark cloud of satanic oppression, orchestrated by the ruling territorial spirit, Maximón. But now that the forces of evil have been pushed back, Almolonga enjoys open heavens, allowing the blessings of God to be poured out. Large, attractive churches are among the most prominent architectural features of the city's hilly landscape.
>
> *Social harmony.* Almolonga was filled with dysfunctional families that were devastated by drunkenness, adultery, wife abuse and child neglect; but now the city is filled with happy marriages, clean homes, wholesome schools and friendly people.
>
> *Material prosperity.* Almolonga no longer suffers poverty caused by chronic drought and famine; now it enjoys agricultural plenty,

producing vegetables that are record-breaking in size. Carrots, for example, are the size of a man's forearm. Crops are now sustained by a natural water supply that comes up from the ground rather than being dependent on rainfall. Farmers deliver their produce throughout Central America in Mercedes trucks that they purchase for cash, christening each one with a Christian name.

Law and order. Until Almolonga was transformed, it had no fewer than six crowded jails to deal with robbery, lawlessness and violence in the streets. Several years ago, however, the last jail was closed because of the absence of crime, and it was turned into a Hall of Honor, which is used for weddings and other celebrations.

Physical and ecological transformation. Almolonga was constantly victimized by plagues, diseases and violent storms. These have now disappeared, while the neighboring city of Zunil, only 3 kilometers away, which still honors the idol of Maximón, remains victimized by those very things.[6]

LEVEL 3—NATION TRANSFORMATION: THE PHILIPPINES

I believe the Philippines has the potential to be the first nation in Asia to become a Christian nation where Christ is Lord and where His kingdom principles and values can fully operate. It has the potential to be a good model if the nation aligns itself to God's principles and purposes. My vision is to see the destiny that God has planned for that nation to come into fulfillment.

The Philippines is a nation filled with natural resources and talented people. It is a beautiful land that is rich and fertile. About fifty years ago, they were the second-most advanced nation in Asia, among the emerging nations of Asia, next only to Japan. Formerly, it was a model for many nations in Asia, with people from South Korea and Malaysia going to the Philippines to learn about education, agriculture, and many other disciplines. World-renowned Filipino artists were winning top awards in international competitions. Filipino singers and musicians have performed in most hotels around the world. Filipinos are adventurous and a people with a spirit of entrepreneurship. The labor force of the Philippines works and serves with excellence and a servant's heart in many nations of the world.

Economic and political crisis

Back then, two Philippine pesos were traded for one US dollar. However, after the reign of former president Marcos, the nation began plunging to near the bottom of the list of developing nations in Asia. At rock bottom level, the pesos were traded in the region of fifty-six pesos to one USD.

According to a 2006 survey by the Population Reference Bureau, 45 percent of the population of the Philippines lived below the poverty line.[7] As revealed in an earlier report by the World Bank, poverty in the Philippines is largely a rural problem, accounting for 79 percent of the world's total poor population. Of these rural poor, two-thirds are in agriculture.[8]

The nation is bleeding from pervasive corruption. Many investors find the Philippines difficult for business ventures. All manner of disasters, whether man-made, natural, or political crises, further hamper economic growth. The Philippines is now at the unenviable bottom rung of developing nations and out of the league of economic dragons and tigers of Asia.

Social crisis

Every year, hundreds of thousands of Filipinos leave their homes to go throughout the world looking for employment as contract workers. Sadly, this includes mothers who leave their children and families behind to earn enough money to provide a better education for their children. This invariably leads to families breaking up, leaving a generation of embittered, rebellious young people who grow up without their mothers nearby. A large pool of professionals and entrepreneurs have joined in the *brain drain* to seek better opportunities for themselves and their children in developed countries such as the United States.

The linking of leaders

Over the years, two Filipino leaders came into my life. One is Eduardo "Eddie" Villanueva, the bishop of Jesus is Lord Church, and the other is Diwa

C. Guinigundo, the current Deputy Governor of the Central Bank of Philippines. Over the years, they have imparted to me a love for The Philippines. I have never seen leaders who have a stronger passion and concern for their nation and people as these two.

I encouraged Brother Eddie to run for the presidency in the 2004 and 2010 elections while he was contemplating on whether to do so. I believe he did the right thing by running, as he created an awareness among God's people to make themselves available in places of influence so as to be in a position to turn the nation around. Both these men have integrity and will not give in to corruption.

In annual surveys by the Makati business community, known as the Wall Street and the most important business district of the Philippines, the Central Bank in the Philippines has been consistently voted as the best performing agency for over ten years. I strongly believe that the church will engage with the government, political leaders, the business community, and other systems of the country in order to transform the nation.

It is my joy to have been able to link Eddie and Diwa together. We must be able to link the right, strategic people together. There is an urgent need for Christian leaders or fathers of the nation, especially leaders of various denominations and ministries, to come together with the purpose of seeing the nation transformed. Our differences should not cloud our goal. It may take ten years or so, but we must begin somewhere. If the leaders and fathers of the nation catch this vision and work together, then the Philippines can possibly be transformed much earlier than a ten-year time frame. We must not allow past wounds and disagreements to get in the way of progress. The leaders of the Philippine churches must show great humility to own this challenge and vision.

Why is it so important for the Philippines to be transformed and realigned with the principles of God's kingdom? It is because this nation can be a model of God's redemptive grace and power.

I believe the Philippines' redemptive gift is to be a nation of servants of God—not as contract workers to serve the household but rather as great servants of God across the nations of the world, serving in various areas of ministries and society. It is supposed to be a missionary nation; their people are adaptable to various cultures and very talented in music and singing as well as information technology and engineering, with a good number working in the Silicon Valley and others with NASA. English is the official language, and it is the largest English-speaking nation in Southeast Asia.

I also believe that it is God's destiny for the Philippines to once again take its place as a leader. As a nation, if its people turn back to God, it would once more be known as a top Asian economic power and a nation where Jesus reigns as Lord. I believe that it is the destiny of this nation for the scourge of poverty to be wiped out in the not-too-distant future; to once again experience economic growth and prosperity, good government, and healthy families. I believe that this nation, under the rulership of God, will be a model nation blessed by God and undergirded by godly men and women in all the spheres of influence in culture.

The Philippines will once again be a beacon to other nations, showing them what Christ can do for a nation when its leaders and people make Him the Lord of their lives and when they allow kingdom principles and values to operate in their spheres of influence.

I believe it is the destiny of the Philippines to experience nation transformation in all the vital sectors of society.

In May 2005, while we were conducting the first conference for nation transformation, under the theme "Touching Heaven, Changing Earth," I believe we sowed the seeds for new changes, including change in currency value. By May 2007 the Philippine peso's value had gone up to 47.6 pesos to one US dollar.

Another example of nation transformation can be seen in the work that has taken place in Canada through the ministry of Watchmen for the Nations under David Demian and Gideon Chiu. They have seen the nation turned around for the Lord. More will be discussed about Canada in chapter 6.

Nation transformation may not happen overnight, but it can begin with just a handful of people; a coalition of the willing and available people who truly want to make a difference and to see God transform their land, people, and country.

CHAPTER 2
THY KINGDOM COME

*M*ost of us, including myself, who have come from an evangelical seminary background typically think in certain fixed mind-sets. However, I along with others have discovered a few common misconceptions about the kingdom of God:

1. *Most people think that the kingdom of God is heaven.* You often hear people say that if we want to enter the kingdom of God or go to heaven, we must first receive Christ. But it is more than just that. The kingdom of God starts right here, right now, while we are on Earth.

2. *The one thousand–year rule of Christ on Earth, the millennial rule:* some people think that the millennial rule is the coming kingdom of God.

3. *The kingdom of God is the church.* The church is the agency of the kingdom, but it does not represent the kingdom in its entirety. The many facets to God's kingdom go beyond church walls and spiritual networks.

In reality the kingdom of God is the rulership of God. George Eldon Ladd, the late professor of biblical theology at Fuller Theological Seminary in Pasadena, California, said, "The Kingdom of God is His kingship, His rule, His authority. When this is once realized, we can go through the New Testament and find passage after passage where this meaning is evident, where the Kingdom is not a realm or a people but God's reign."[1]

Jesus said, "Behold, the kingdom of God is here." Jesus became the first person in whom the kingdom of God came. Jesus embodied the kingdom of God; the personification of the kingdom of God was seen in Him. God directed every aspect of Jesus's life. God desires His rulership to extend to all communities, societies, and the cities on this Earth. God's people are the agency, messengers, and catalysts of this change so that God's rulership can be established.

THE ORIGINAL MANDATE

Right from day one of man's creation, God had given His mandate to man. In Genesis 1:26, He told Adam and Eve to have dominion over all the earth, which some call "dominion theology." Some evangelicals react strongly against the concept of ruling over the earth.

However, we cannot have merely an evangelistic mandate that limits our mission exclusively to preaching the gospel while we disengage ourselves from business, government, and society. Genesis 1:26 states that we have a cultural mandate to rule and take authority over all the creatures of this world.

What is the original mandate that God gave us?

> God blessed them, and God said to them, "Be fruitful and multiply; fill the earth and subdue it; have dominion over the fish of the sea, over the birds of the air, and over every living thing that moves on the earth."
> —GENESIS 1:28

The original mandate was not only to be fruitful and multiply but to have dominion over the earth. That means we have responsibility and authority over the nations, cities, communities, and even the environment of this earth. We cannot shy away from politics, government, business, or society.

After God gave that mandate to Adam, an individual, God also gave a similar mandate to Abraham:

> I will make you a great nation; I will bless you and make your name great; and you shall be a blessing. I will bless those who bless you, and I will curse him who curses you; and in you all the families of the earth shall be blessed.
> —GENESIS 12:2–3

When God gave this mandate to Abraham, His intent was that Abraham's family would be a model of His rulership being manifest on earth. God's family in heaven is able to be manifested on earth through Abraham's family. During the time of Abraham, when the people were distant from God, He was known as the God of heaven and earth. In contrast, each time Abraham built an altar, he declared the rulership of God over his life, and God began to reveal Himself as the Yahweh once more. He is Lord of Abraham and that region.

Then, through Isaac, his son Jacob, and Jacob's twelve sons, God brought forth a nation called Israel. The nation of Israel was intended to be a prototype of God's rulership on earth. The purpose of Israel was that it would be the masterpiece of God and His display model for other nations to see and also desire God's rulership. The effect generally should have been for other nations to sit up and say to Israel, "Yes, I want to live like that too! Can we have God to rule over us as He rules over you?"

The children of Israel were meant to be a people who would know God and be ruled by Him, having joy, blessings, prosperity, life, and vitality. However, we read that Israel became proud, arrogant, rebellious, and disobedient; therefore, God's purpose could not be accomplished through them. God sent prophets like Jeremiah, Ezekiel, Isaiah, and many others to tell them where they had gone wrong and to repent lest God's judgment would come upon them. Sadly, they did not listen and went through two series of judgments— the Assyrian captivity and the Babylonian captivity.

Our original mandate is to establish God's rulership on this earth.

THE KINGDOM OF GOD

In the days of Daniel, God gave a dream to Nebuchadnezzar. Isn't this amazing? A secular king wanted to know what was going to happen in the future, and God granted him his desire, revealing the future to him.

Throughout history, four types of empires or kingdoms existed as examples of God's intended rulership.

The Gold Kingdom

The first empire to collapse was the Babylonian empire, where the king's rule was supreme. Represented by gold, it reflects the highest of what God intends and where He should rule as King over the kingdoms of men.

The Silver Kingdom

Then the Medes-Persian empire came, where the rule of law was supreme. It was so supreme that even the king could not change the laws. That is why when Daniel was thrown into the lion's den, the king could do nothing but cry to God that he would be preserved. This empire is represented by silver.

The Bronze Kingdom

The third empire was the Greek empire. Brought into being by Alexander the Great and represented by bronze, military rule was supreme. Some nations today are patterned after this, such as Thailand (August 2011 reverted back to democratic election), Fiji, and certain parts of South America and Africa where the military has stepped in to take over the government of the nation. However, the bronze kingdom is inferior to the silver kingdom, where law is supreme. That is why there is always a cry for the rule of law and enactment of the constitution.

The Iron Kingdom

Then the Roman empire came—represented by iron—where the rule of civil government was supreme. This is the predominant type of government today. The Roman empire collapsed, of course, after the persecution brought by the Roman emperors from Nero to Diocletian. God began to move in such a way that the entire Roman empire became Christian when worship was legalized through the Edict of Milan issued by Constantine in AD 313.

During the Iron Kingdom period of time, people have started to speculate on what is the fifth empire that is to come before Christ comes again. Made of iron and clay, it could be a mixture of some kind of Roman empire, but it is brittle and will collapse. Some speculate that this is the European Union (EU). At one time, the goal was for ten member states. But now the number of members in the EU is exceeding that goal, so there is some confusion in the system.

But as far as God is concerned, the kingdoms of men will always fall because it is His kingdom that He wants to establish.

> In the days of these kings the God of heaven will set up a kingdom which shall never be destroyed; and the kingdom shall not be left to

other people; it shall break in pieces and consume all these kingdoms, and it shall stand forever.

—DANIEL 2:44

World-class empires will not last, as we have seen throughout history. The kingdom of God will break these down. In the midst of world empires during Daniel's time, God established His rulership. Every government must align itself with the rulership of God or face destruction.

Our mandate is to establish God's rulership on this earth. Let us align ourselves to His kingdom principles so that the nations will be able to achieve the destiny that God has for them. This is the desire that we have for Malaysia and the nation of the Philippines as well as many other nations. Our vision is not a nation filled with poverty and corruption, but one that is aligned with godly principles and values and experiencing blessings in all aspects.

PARABLES OF THE KINGDOM

The purposes of the kingdom of God can be seen throughout the Bible from the Old Testament to the New Testament. God is interested not only in the salvation of souls. Over and beyond that, He is more interested to see the kingdom of God come into a person's life. Through a people who seek to do His will, God's rulership can be fully manifested in their lives. They can become effective instruments for extending the kingdom of God so that it becomes pervasive in both culture and society. Like the leaven that Jesus speaks of, the kingdom of God can work to transform the entire nation, at every level of government and in every sphere of culture. Even if it begins with just a few individuals, God can turn things around and cause people to see what heaven on earth should be like.

HOW SHOULD WE PRAY?

Jesus taught us to pray that the kingdom of God would come unto this earth and that His will be done on earth as it is in heaven. What does it mean to pray for His kingdom and His will to come to earth as it is in heaven? What is in heaven? Prosperity, peace, joy, the presence of God, righteousness, love, life, mercy, and justice. These are vital attributes for the nations of the earth.

Jesus taught many parables about the kingdom of God, and He preached that the kingdom of God was at hand. In the same way that God used Israel in the Old Testament, He now works through the church in the New Testament. The difference is that in the Old Testament, Israel was meant to draw people to come and see what God was doing in Israel; but in the New Testament, the church is meant to go out into the world in order to bring in the people.

In Matthew 13, Jesus taught about the kingdom of God through a number of parables other than the parable of the leaven. The parable of the sower speaks about God's desire to establish His rulership over our lives and for us to be fruitful one hundredfold. Jesus taught in parables about the influence of the kingdom that is like the mustard seed growing into a big tree. The kingdom of God is the rule of God, first established in our lives, then extended to communities, cities, and nations. Jesus was the first and best embodiment of the kingdom of God within a human life.

THE TRUE PURPOSE OF GOD'S KINGDOM

God wants to bring down heaven on earth. This is not about an after-death experience. Heaven begins here and now. He wants to bring His people back to Him, so that they begin to worship Him as King and fulfill His purposes for the nations of the world as it is in heaven. God desires that heaven come down on earth so that heaven and earth become one. The agency is God's people, the church. This is consistent with the acts of the prophets in the Old Testament and the message they gave. Isaiah, Hosea, Micah, Elijah, Jeremiah, Ezekiel—they all preached about righteousness, injustice, godliness, repentance, and turning back to God.

Many of us find it hard to read about the Old Testament prophets because we don't understand them. However, if you understand the purpose of God's kingdom, then you will also understand the message of the prophets. They are consistent in talking about God, bringing Him back to His people, His righteousness, peace, and rulership upon the nations of the world. If you can see that aspect, you are able to see the heart of God, the cry of God for His people to come back to Him and for the nations to crown Him as Lord.

Look at the Great Commission. What did Jesus really mean when He asked us to make disciples of all nations? Ralph Winters translated the word *nations* as "people groups" or "ethnic groups." But *nations* can also mean sovereign states; therefore, it refers to people groups such as the Selako, Iban,

Kadazan, Chinese, Indians, Malays, and dozens more ethnic groups of Malaysia. But that doesn't negate the fact that *nations* can also refer to countries such as China, India, Australia, and so forth. We cannot disregard that fact, or we will be inconsistent. So, Jesus's perspective on discipleship is not just individualistic. He never saw discipleship as confined to individuals only. It was also intended for entire communities and sovereign states.

REDEMPTIVE GIFTS

To see the nations bow down to Jesus Christ, to ask the King of heaven to rule on earth—that was the mandate for God's people. God is interested in seeing every nation fulfill its destiny.

Each nation has its own redemptive gift and unique destiny, designed to fulfill a specific calling for God. For example, Cindy Jacobs prophesied that Malaysia's destiny is to be a nation for missions. Malaysia's main redemptive gift is unity and harmony in a multicultural society. Another of Malaysia's redemptive gifts in terms of its economy is banking. We have some redemptive gifts in the form of commodities like oil and other resources.

Malaysia has a specific spiritual calling as a nation. Malaysia is destined to become a model nation, but a model of which kingdom? *God's kingdom or some other kingdom?* We have a choice. Let us try to make the right one for the sake of future generations.

The kingdom of God is an ongoing process that will reach its optimum only when Christ comes again to rule the earth. Until He comes, Jesus will not only free people from demons, heal the sick, and save the lost, but He also desires to see communities transformed and set free from poverty, oppression, injustice, and corruption. At the same time, He wants to see us enjoying blessings, prosperity, peace, joy, and a good government. Blessed is the nation whose God is the Lord!

THE CRITICAL MASS

Nobody knows the critical mass for changes to happen. When Abraham interceded for Sodom and Gomorrah with the intent that the Lord would not destroy that city for its corruption, the critical mass at that time could have been ten people, or perhaps just one. But Abraham did not know what the minimum was at that time, and we may never know what is the critical mass needed to transform our society, government, or nation. But God knows. It could be thousands, only ten, or possibly just two. None of us will ever know, so let us not be the guilty one to stand back and watch the critical mass being deprived of just one more to make the difference.

But count on it: God is looking for major changes to take place for this century in nations of the world!

GOD LOVES ALL NATIONS

What are the problems in the Middle East? Well, the biblical promises for these nations need to be considered. The Bible tells us we war not against flesh and blood but against spiritual forces of darkness (Eph. 6:12). These issues are approached not from a political perspective but a spiritual perspective; not fighting against political ideologies or against any particular people group, nor even elements of religious extremism, but against the powers and principalities of darkness. Neither the Arabs, Persians, nor Jews are the enemy but the demonic forces that are battling for rulership over those nations.

The root of all these things goes right back to the time of Abraham. When he received the word of God about a son, he tried to fulfill that word by having a child through Hagar, his wife's Egyptian handmaid. During that time it was culturally acceptable to do so, but that was not the way that God intended the promise to be fulfilled. Because Abraham was anxious for an heir, he acted in the flesh and went his own human way to see the promises take shape by taking Hagar as his concubine and conceiving Ishmael.

Sarah became upset by Hagar's attitude. Hagar despised Sarah. In Genesis 16:6, Abraham told Sarah to do whatever she wanted with Hagar. This is where we see that Abraham should have accepted much of the blame, and not just Sarah. Sarah dealt so harshly with Hagar that she fled. But then the angel met Hagar in the desert and called her to return and submit herself under the authority of Sarah. In Genesis 17:19–21, we see that God promises to greatly bless the descendants of Ishmael.

> I will also make a nation of the son of the bondwoman, because he is your seed.
> —GENESIS 21:13

God did not leave out Ishmael but promised to bless Ishmael because he was also Abraham's offspring. The Palestinians and the Arabs today are both from the seed of Abraham.

Several years ago in a meeting at Washington DC with Cindy Jacobs, an intercessor from Kuwait but of Egyptian descent suddenly stood up on behalf of his people. He was weeping away, and said, "I was just seventeen years old when my father Abraham pushed me away, threw me out, and left me to die in the desert." Because of rejection by Abraham and by Sarah—but mostly by the father—the hurt was there from the beginning. Hatred had grown against the sons of Isaac and from being rejected by the family. If only Abraham and Sarah had accepted and loved Ishmael as a son despite the mistake they had made, much enmity and hatred could have been avoided today. _Do you know that many raised in Arab lands were taught to hate the Jews and Israel?_ Extremism is birthed from hatred and rejection.

Another intercessor from Israel, Ari Sorko-Ram who is the son-in-law of the deceased Gordon Lindsay, a well-known theologian and the founder of Christ for the Nations, stood on behalf of Abraham to ask for forgiveness for rejecting such a young boy, and to receive him as a brother. It was a very moving act of identification repentance between two great peoples.

RECONCILIATION, TRANSFERENCE OF WEALTH, AND WORSHIP OF ONE TRUE GOD

God is God of all nations. He loves all nations. He doesn't choose the Israelites alone as if they are an elite nation, the only people that God will love. They are supposed to be a model and example for others to follow, not an exclusive nation.

During that same meeting in Washington DC, we carried out many identification repentance acts between representatives from Israel and the Arab nations. We believe that what is done in the spiritual realm will have repercussions in the political realm.

Look at some of the promises in Isaiah 60:7 that have yet to be fulfilled. Kedar and Nebaioth were sons of Ishmael, patriarchs of this nation. Genesis 25:12–14 lists down the genealogy of Ishmael's descendants. Isaiah 60:7 says that the flocks of Kedar will gather to Israel, and that the rams of Nebaioth will minister to Israel. Their worship will be accepted by God. Let us believe that this prophetic word will come to pass and that one day in the future, reconciliation between these people groups will take place.

It is interesting to note that after Sarah died, Abraham married Keturah and had sons with her. Before Abraham died, he gave gifts to the sons of Keturah and sent them away to the East, far from Isaac (Gen. 25:6). One of the sons was Midian, the father of the Midianites. Other descendants went to Persia, now known as Iran, while others went to Assyria, the empire that includes modern day Iraq. Isaiah 60:8 asks, "Who are these people?" These are the sons and grandchildren of Keturah and Abraham. Ephah and Sheba were grandsons. The verse says that they would bring gold and incense. *Could these be the wise men from the East who brought the gold, myrrh, and frankincense to Jesus at His birth?* Gold speaks of transference of wealth, and incense speaks of worship. I believe that someday these nations will experience the worship of the one true God, and that transference of wealth will take place for both for Iran and Iraq.

> In that day there will be an altar to the LORD in the midst of the land of Egypt, and a pillar to the LORD at its border. And it will be for a sign and for a witness to the LORD of hosts in the land of Egypt; for they will cry to the LORD because of the oppressors, and He will send them a Savior and a Mighty One, and He will deliver them. Then the LORD will be known to Egypt, and the Egyptians will know the LORD in that day, and will make sacrifice and offering; yes, they will make a vow to the LORD and perform it.
>
> —ISAIAH 19:19–21

God will send a messenger to Egypt proclaiming a new covenant and bring a spiritual revival to Abraham's descendants.

> In that day there will be a highway from Egypt to Assyria, and the Assyrian will come into Egypt and the Egyptian into Assyria, and the Egyptians will serve with the Assyrians. In that day Israel will be one of three with Egypt and Assyria—a blessing in the midst of the land, whom the LORD of hosts shall bless, saying, "Blessed is Egypt My people, and Assyria the work of My hands, and Israel My inheritance."
>
> —ISAIAH 19:23–25

Egypt, Iraq, and Israel will be a blessing in the midst of the land. Who would have believed some years ago that Iraq could be transformed? However, now it is easier to believe. That would not have been possible if not for the change of leadership in Iraq. The prophetic word is coming to pass before our very eyes. It is time for us to take our place in intercession and pray for the promises of God. We need to contend for all that has yet to be fulfilled to come to pass, even in our lifetime.

Let us not be filled with hatred or despise any group of people. Let there be peace, reconciliation, transference of wealth, and the worship of the one true God.

CHAPTER 3
DEALING WITH MIND-SETS

*M*OST PEOPLE HAVE a fixed way of thinking. Their mind-set and perception of things can be hard to change after being molded by years of family upbringing, social influence, and personal experiences. Many times it is easier to follow the traditional way of doing things.

Our mind-set determines our decisions and how we see things. Picture this analogy: If I were to use different colored sunglasses or viewing devices to look at the same object, it would look different each time I used any of them at different occasions. The piece of white paper before me looks pink through red sunglasses; looks blurry if my glasses were underpowered; looks magnified if I viewed it through a pair of binoculars. How the object appears would depend on what I decide to view it with for that particular instance.

Likewise, for nation transformation to take place, the way we perceive certain things must change. However, we must first come to an understanding in order to identify the various mental barriers that could possibly prevent us from nation transformation.

At least seven types of mind-set conditions need to be addressed:

1. Mind-Set of the Separation between Church and State

2. The Stained Glass Mind-Set vs. the Marketplace Mind-Set

3. Mind-Set of Withdrawal vs. Engaging

4. Escapism Mind-Set vs. Kingdom Mind-Set

5. Poverty Mind-Set vs. Prosperity Mind-Set

6. Local Church Mind-Set vs. Kingdom Mind-Set

7. Negative Mind-Set vs. Positive Mind-Set

1. Mind-Set of Separation between Church and State

The origins of the separation *mind-set*

Frequently, churches do not want to be involved in business, government, or any secular activity. This philosophy was advocated by Englishman John Locke (1632–1704) but took root in America. Generally traced to Thomas Jefferson,[1] the concept was that the government would not adopt an official religious belief for the people. Since then, this concept, known as the Wall of Separation of Church and State, has been adopted by several countries.

In today's society the mind-set flows through seminaries and other training institutions, so much so that churches do not want to be involved at all. This mind-set of separation of church and state is rooted in platonic dualism, which teaches that the church and state should not mix. Here, the idea of the church refers to spiritual things such as piety, faith, heaven and hell, and so forth; whereas politics, government, and business are the domain of the state. Western society is built upon this idea.[2]

This mind-set of separation was further reinforced because of bad experiences that the church in Europe had when the power of the church was stronger than the state. In AD 800 Pope Leo III ordained Charlemagne as *Imperator Romanorum*, literally "Emperor of the Romans," a title reserved for the emperor of the Western Roman empire.[3] With the rise of the papacy power, the church had a huge influence over the government.[4]

The Spanish Inquisition was notorious for torturing so-called heretics to force them to renounce their beliefs. The fear of the church dominating the government was genuine and experienced by those in Europe.[5] At the same time, the Pilgrims, persecuted for their separatist beliefs, fled from England and the Anglican Church, eventually settling in America. They detested the state's control over the church and believed it could result in persecution. They wanted to form a democracy in which the people had the freedom to worship as they pleased and all religious beliefs would be tolerated. These Separatist Puritans—who were evangelicals—strongly fought for their own religious freedom and refused authority of the pope or even the head of the state church.[6] They wanted a clear separation between church and government.

A great misinterpretation of the Constitution

After the Constitution of America was first drafted, many people thought that the First Amendment endorsed the idea of separation of church and state. However, this was not the case!

It was Thomas Jefferson who first coined the term "separation of church and state." He had meant it in the context of the government not interfering with the affairs of the church. It was never meant that prayer should be taken out of schools. In those days, they even had a church in the capitol for congressmen and senators.

Hope Taylor, who serves as director of the International Leadership Embassy in Washington DC, once spoke on how the phrase "separation of church and state" originally came about. This was how he put it:

> The phrase, "separation of Church and State" came from a letter written by one of the presidents of the US, Thomas Jefferson. In that letter in 1802 to Baptists in Danbury, Connecticut, Jefferson wrote a phrase saying of "a wall of separation between the church and the state." Jefferson was paraphrasing the words of a famous Baptist, Roger Williams who spoke of a wall being needed to protect the church from government interference. Jefferson believed that the Constitution's First Amendment was a legal wall that prevented the national government from setting up a favored national church. Jefferson did support the separation of Church and State, but to him, this meant that there would be no single official state-favored denomination supported by tax dollars.
>
> Two days after he wrote that letter, in Jan 3, 1802, he went for the first time to a church service held in the House Chamber at the Capitol building, a government building of the United States of America. As a president, a civil servant and leader of the land, he faithfully attended three church meetings constantly for the next seven years. He believed that religious expression in the public sector was not prohibited by the Constitution. While he opposed government compulsion of religion, he supported government involvement in religion in many ways.
>
> Here are some examples of how Jefferson encouraged religious expression:

- Supported legislative and military chaplains. The chaplain of the US Senate is a spirit-filled man who knows the Word of God, preaches it and has an awesome anointing upon his life.

- Recommended a national seal using religious symbols.

- Appointed official days of fasting and prayer.

- Wrote laws punishing Sabbath breakers.

- Supported the use of Christian oaths.

- Allowed government property and facilities to be used for worship.

- Supported the use of the Bible and non-denominational religious instruction in public schools.

- Funding of salaries of clergymen in Indian mission schools.

- Exempting churches from taxation.

Jefferson recognized the great need for Christian religion to be dispersed throughout a nation that desires to be free. He contributed personally throughout his life to the Bible Society. In 1814, he sent money to one Bible society saying, "I had not supposed that there was a family in this state that did not possess a Bible. I therefore enclose you cheerfully an order for 50 dollars for the purpose of the society."

While President Jefferson served as Chairman of the DC school board from 1805–1807, he promoted the teaching of the Bible in the public schools of Washington DC. He said, "The Bible is the cornerstone of liberty. A student's perusal of the sacred volume will make him a better citizen, a better father and a better husband."

The First Amendment of the Constitution of the United States: "Congress shall make no law respecting an establishment of religion or prohibiting the free exercise thereof." This is the amendment that so many liberals use to support their belief that there should be some separation between Church and State. But it doesn't say anything about a wall or separation where the state and religion don't intermingle or interface. There is nothing in the legal documents of the US that says that.[7]

Over the years, missionaries and church leaders from Western civilization who went to other parts of the world such as Asia began teaching in Bible schools and seminaries about the need for separation of church and state. "The church should only be involved in spiritual things," they would pronounce. "Stay far away from involvement with the government!"

This outlook must change now! The church must engage with the government. Though the churches do not interfere in the administration of the government, the church has to take its role of being the conscience of the government. We have a prophetic role to fulfill in our nations.

It is a major mental block that must be removed. The church should not be *political* but *governmental*. The objective here is not to overthrow but to ensure justice and fair values in places of authority. This means that instead of favoring one party over another, our role should be to stand for God's kingdom and to see that those who run for offices—including the legislative, judiciary, or executive positions—will stand on God's side and align their values and principles with those of God's kingdom.

Righteousness and justice for all can only come from upright and fair decision makers. Whatever their party or political stand, candidates who uphold God's principles must be supported and empowered to do good things for the nation when they are placed in positions of power and influence. Most importantly, they should be God-fearing men and women of integrity who are not to be corrupted for personal gain.

The younger generation should equip themselves, study hard, develop skills, and pursue the right kind of training to position themselves as potential members of parliament, state assemblymen, the judiciary or other governmental agencies. This is something crucial, and we should pray for them and support them in this area.

2. The Stained-Glass Mind-Set vs. the Marketplace Mind-Set

A common mind-set among churches holds that ministry is only functional within the church. But what about our daily lives and activities?

Every day we go to work, do business, go to school, buy things, and interact and engage with various facets of society. Ministry must not just be confined to the four walls of the church. We must change our stained-glass mind-set so that we can begin to enable the majority of God's people to do great things for Him in our time and generation. We need many individuals to occupy key strategic positions in every level of society to bring about change.

When we think that we can only minister within the church, we will never make any impact or change our communities. See it beyond the church walls. Going out to work every day is ministry. Attending college is ministry. Conducting a business is ministry. Serving in various areas of government is ministry. Where we are at, where we are positioned, and what we have been appointed to be—*that* is our ministry.

The role of marketplace apostles

What releases the marketplace is the revelation concerning workplace or marketplace apostles. The sad thing is that the church is not geared for this change. Many are not even open to what God is saying at this time. To understand the role of marketplace apostles, let us revisit some church and biblical history.

During the era of the 1970s, the prayer movement swept across the globe. Intercessors are the ones to stand in the gap and pray for God to move on the people. Francis Frangipane makes this statement: "The 'gap' is the distance between the way things are and the way things should be" and that it is the responsibility of godly leaders to make sure the gap gets filled.[8] During the 1980s, God released the office of the prophet with the role of hearing and speaking the word of God and its revelation. With the 1990s, the office of the apostle was released in a powerful way so that God's government, completed by the apostles, could be positioned. So, how do we see each of these roles contributing to strengthening the church and fitting together in one piece?

Sociologists talk about nuclear families and extended families. Let us draw a parallel with the church. If we have the nuclear church, with corporate meetings for Sunday worship, Bible studies, and other activities; and the extended church, with meetings five or six days a week in the workplace; then the church would consist of not just those who meet on Sundays at the local church, but those who meet elsewhere as well. Therefore, if there are apostles in the church, logic tells us that there are apostles in the workplace too.

Daniel was an apostle; he was not a priest. Joseph was neither a priest nor a prophet, but a role model for a marketplace apostle. Yet God directed their lives into government, and He moved them into the prophetic realm as well. Esther was never a priest, but as the Jewish queen of the Persian king Ahasuerus, she was able to influence the change of laws when she fasted and prayed for favor.

We are living in a time when there must be workplace apostles. Throughout biblical times, God has been bringing about nation transformation through people of this calling: Joseph in government as prime minister; David in government as king of Israel; Nehemiah in government service as the cup bearer to the king; Daniel, a district governor and government official, whom the king had in mind to make prime minister over all his provinces and over all the other government officials. Consider Joshua, the military commander who led the children of Israel across Jordan and into the Promised Land. These were the people who transformed nations and societies—the marketplace apostles of their time, fulfilling God's purposes and changing many people's destinies.

Two important functions are crucial to marketplace or workplace apostles:

+ National and Social Transformation
+ Transference of Wealth

Since we have touched on the function of the marketplace apostles in the national and social transformation, the transference of wealth must be addressed.

Transference of wealth

God's kingdom efforts will require finances to break the spirit of poverty over nations. Peter Wagner made an eye-opening statement when he said that transfer of wealth is vital for nation transformation.[9] As we study Scripture with that thought in mind, we can see how the practical aspects of wealth transference are critical for transformation.

> God gives wisdom and knowledge and joy to a man who is good in
> His sight; but to the sinner He gives the work of gathering and col-
> lecting, that he may give to him who is good before God.
> —ECCLESIASTES 2:26

God takes the wealth of the unrighteous and transfers it to His people (Prov. 13:22). The finances He gives are not for us to lavish upon ourselves but for kingdom projects and efforts to break the spirit of poverty. If we want our businesspeople to succeed, we must pray for them to see that wealth is to be used for kingdom purposes and not just for their enjoyment. If we can understand and act on that principle, we can then see tremendous transference of wealth taking place. We are living in times when a rapid and great transference of wealth is going to take place. Global shaking and economical upheavals are forcing hundreds of millions of dollars and resources to change hands. As good stewards of the resources given to us, we need to quickly strategize and plan what we should do with the finances before time runs out.

A major shift in the way people give is going to take place; from donor-based giving to revenue-based giving. In the past, giving to missions meant donating to missionaries, projects, ministries, or the poor. However, that type of giving is only meant for a short-term gap. If you give a million dollars to a beggar, he might end up owing $10 million, especially if he's a gambler! Instead, eliminate poverty by giving the people a model for farming, manufacturing, or business. So the saying goes: "Give a man a fish and you feed him for a day. Teach a man to fish and you feed him for a lifetime" (author unknown).

For example, establish a program for microloans for the impoverished, and give training to learn some business expertise and skills. Provide mentoring for success. Funds that are provided must go into projects that can continuously generate revenue on their own. Just giving money causes it to run out, and needs keep increasing. When the ministries grow, more money is needed. Endless needs are the result.

Organizations such as Opportunity International, Hope International, and World Vision see improvements in housing and access to health care. Income and net business profits are increasing. Empowerment, self-esteem, decision-making ability, community participation, and leadership increase. According to the Nobel Peace Committee, "Development from below also serves to advance democracy and human rights. Microcredit has proved to be an important liberating force in societies where women, in particular, have to struggle against repressive social and economic conditions."[10]

Marketplace apostles must seek strategies from God about how to empower the impoverished. This may be extremely difficult in areas of the world where the enemies of the gospel will make accusations, such as accusing them of making unethical conversions.

An Australian foundation is helping the poor in Tanzania by supplying solar-powered lights. Many villages in Tanzania have no power supply, and many homes use kerosene lamps for light. This is costly as well as dangerous as it may burn down the house, and it is not environmentally friendly. The foundation devised a strategy to provide solar-powered devices that are brighter than the kerosene lamps that are being replaced, and they cost approximately the same amount as four months' fuel for the kerosene lamp. The lights have a lifespan of five years. This brings a huge cost savings to the villages and is much safer and environmentally friendly. The foundation has three concepts for success: affordability, quality, and usability. An additional benefit is that the venture is profitable for the foundation.

Fighting poverty: the strategic way

Revenue-based projects rather than donor-based projects bring a better result. Don't just give a fish. Teach how to fish, so the recipients are able to earn a decent living.

Wealth is available to fight poverty in many underdeveloped nations and developing nations, including the Philippines. But this time, it comes with a difference. Instead of providing food, shelter, and basic needs to the poor, let us introduce certain business models for entrepreneurs so that they can learn to create wealth rather than depend upon handouts. Provide funds for startup capital to operate mixed farming or other livelihoods to help provide their basic needs. Funds are allowed for start-up capital. Funds can also be strategically channeled toward providing expertise, management skills, personnel training, and equipment.

Now, the paradigm shift will be for people to start giving toward a business project in order to generate revenue from those funds. Ultimately, those profits can be used to sponsor all the ministry projects without eating into the capital.

Foundations established with assets that generate revenue for distribution to philanthropic and charitable organizations are a good example of ongoing investment into people and communities. Many times foundations are established for the purpose of education, investment into new technologies and other inventions, and investment into entrepreneurs who are establishing start-up ventures and other long-term investments toward future generations.

3. MIND-SET OF WITHDRAWAL VS. ENGAGING

Most Christians do not want to be involved with the world. Because of erroneous teachings and traditions, they may feel that the world is wicked and sinful. However, in Matthew 11:19 Jesus is accused of eating with tax collectors and sinners. Jesus was actually actively engaging with the market-place of His time.

According to Mark 5, Jesus left Galilee and went to the country of the Gadarenes, a place where the Gentiles lived. This is where miracles and healings abound. When Jesus crossed the sea and stepped out of the boat, He immediately encountered the demonic man. Then He told that man to go home to Decapolis to proclaim the great things that Jesus had done for him. Decapolis was ten cities inhabited by the Greeks. Jesus modeled this and many other examples for believers so they would understand how to live their lives.

In the second century of the history of the church, godly men who aspired to be spiritual began leading ascetic lives. Thus began the monastic movement with its hallmark of participants renouncing worldly goods, wealth, and life. When monasteries were developed, they attracted many, including nobility, the wealthy, and family men. Whether they were living as individual hermits or in monasteries, monks dedicated themselves to self-denial and withdrawal from the world mind-set in order to be spiritual rather than engaging with the world. Their reaction to the growing laxity within the church caused them to seek after renewal that later became missionary movements. These lay movements attracted great followings, but their desire to become more spiritual led them into withdrawing from practical daily living and from the world. Jesus did not withdraw from the world but was intimately involved with people and their lives.

When Francis of Assisi's father took him before the bishop to disinherit him, Francis stripped himself of the clothing that was on him and, standing naked before the bishop, declared that henceforth he desired to serve only "our Father which art in heaven."[11] Thus these monastic movements that spread over many centuries became a model for many sincere people. The model was that for one to attain greater spiritual life, one has to withdraw from the world. Yet there are also those that aspire to live in Christian communities for the same reason. God's purpose is for His people not to be isolated from the world but to be insulated from its bad influence. We are to be the light of the world, meaning we are positioned by God to influence the world with right living and values. We are also the salt to preserve it from the decay that results from corrupt and evil practices.

In our generation God's people are also withdrawing from engaging the world. If we do not position God's people into places of influence in government and encourage our young people to move into politics, then by default we have surrendered the running of the country to men and women who may not have a strong moral and godly foundation. This is an open door for them to be easily corrupted and lust for power.

Rene Q. Bas, a columnist for a Philippine newspaper, lamented that the World Bank's release of its 2008 Worldwide Governance Indicators of 212 countries showed that the Philippines was now at the bottom of the list in fighting corruption among the ten largest East Asian economies.[12] The Philippines has the dubious distinction of being lesser in rank than Indonesia and way below Asia's best-ranking countries; Singapore and Hong Kong, Taiwan and South Korea are the best scorers overall for good governance, not just for the control of corruption.

Then Bas remarked, "The pervasiveness of government corruption in this country [the Philippines] is nothing less than mysterious. Most of the high officials are Christians. But many of them who hold the highest offices lie at every turn. They steal. They make a mockery of the Catholic Christianity they love to identify themselves with in photo ops. Their actions tear to shreds their oaths of office, the Constitution and the ordinances of the land."[13] This shows that being called Christians is not good enough; we need to have men and women like Daniel and his friends to purpose in their hearts not to defile themselves when they are yet young (see Daniel 1:8).

In the United States, a Baptist church called for a boycott on Disneyland for its infusion of witchery influence. Instead, why can't Christian businessmen invest in Disneyland and the affiliates of the Walt Disney Company and own a majority holding so that they can influence the direction, values, and policies of the company?

In Australia, Christian parents are concerned that their children are watching some of the popular TV programs filled with infidelity and lax morality and that they are being influenced by such values. In one of my meetings in the Gold Coast region with a group of businessmen and a city councilor, I challenged them to buy a majority stake in one of the leading TV channels. One of them, CEO of Paladin Group Dave Hodgson, thanked me for bringing the matter up, as he took what I shared as confirmation of the same challenge God had spoken to him. He had driven more than two hours from Sunshine Coast.

Christian schools are doing well in Australia; they have a long waiting list. Though this is commendable as a model, we should not withdraw our influence from the public schools. Rightly, God's people should be positioned in all aspects of the education system in order to influence its policy, curriculum, and direction. It is in these public schools that the majority of the children are receiving their educations. We should encourage our young people to be teachers and lecturers in schools and institutions of learning. Parents should be engaged in parent-teacher associations. This is because education is one of the important sectors of society that shape the future leaders of the nation.

4. ESCAPISM MIND-SET VS. KINGDOM MIND-SET

Some people believe in the end-time teaching that Christ is coming soon. "So why work hard, earn money, or build houses? Let's just wait for Christ to come soon, and preach the gospel. That's all there is to life." It makes one apathetic and complacent about achieving the best for God.

The other mind-set is that Christ will rule on earth for a millennium. "Therefore, let us just endure this world that is full of problems and sufferings for a while, wipe away our tears, and by and by we will escape from the sufferings of this world." That is not the correct mind-set! Jesus wants us to establish the kingdom of God on earth, not to flee or disassociate from it. We need to fully grasp and understand the true concept of the kingdom of God so that we can effect change on earth.

Some of these end-time teachings can cause us to have an escapism mind-set. Instead of focusing our efforts on improving things here and now, we become more obsessed about not being left behind than getting ready for Christ, who is coming soon!

The escapism mind-set was first established in the concept of the Rapture of the church. This idea initially appeared in commentaries in the 1700s but was popularized in the early 1800s by John Nelson Darby, who is considered the father of dispensationalism. In the early 1900s, the Scofield Reference Bible further promoted the idea. The fruit of such false teaching—which has been taught for almost two hundred years—is often short-term thinking rather than establishing the kingdom of God.

Church, what is your plan?

I was involved in the AD2000 and Beyond Movement and other similar movements. An underlying eschatological position in all these movements was that Christ would come by the year 2000, or at most 2004. But what if that eschatological position was wrong and Christ did not come by then? Because of that, as a church, we didn't have a plan for the future. This was especially true when we approached AD 2000–2004, because many believed that Christ would return by then. They didn't have a plan for the future years because the plan was that Jesus would be coming soon anyway. Some even have talked about how the Antichrist has been revealed in Syria, and that Christ is coming soon.

The kingdom of God is coming with power and violence to take back from the devil what is ours, and there will be transformation of the nations and even creation itself.

The "Jesus is coming soon" eschatology looks at life as if our lives now are hard, causing us to desire to wait for the Millennium and a future utopia. This is escapism and not facing up to reality. I do not dispute the reality of the second coming of Christ. Actually, Jesus, when speaking of His second coming, commanded us to "occupy or do business" till He comes:

> So he called ten of his servants and gave them ten minas. "Put this money to work," he said, "until I come back."
> —LUKE 19:13, NIV

In the New Testament it says the kingdom of this world will become the kingdom of our Lord. The kingdom of God is coming with power and violence to take back from the devil what is ours, and there will be transformation of the nations and even creation itself. Redemption will come to creation when the sons of God begin to emerge and God begins to transform His church and the nations, and even the environment. This is a very powerful teaching from the New Testament. That is the way we should be thinking so that we have a future agenda that extends through many generations.

Today, God is beginning to release new strategies for us to achieve our future agenda, which includes the kingdoms of this world becoming His kingdom. These strategies involve marketplace apostles, nation transformation, kingdom dominion theology, new models to reach cities through megachurches, and new models for missions that have been limited by donor-based giving being replaced by revenue-based funds where businesses can be set up to support missional projects.

A powerful synergy of businesses and ministries will experience many more breakthroughs in changing nations and societies than just ministries going it alone. Networking among ministries and bringing down dividing church walls are keys to changes. If the Communist structure came down within seventy years, so can all other structures. Nothing is impossible if God's people will come together as one.

When and how Christ comes is *none of our business*. To enable the kingdom of Christ to come on earth *is our business*. We should have targets of at least ten to fifteen years, but a better plan is for an entire generation.

5. POVERTY MIND-SET VS. PROSPERITY MIND-SET

Similar to the mind-set of separation of church and state, the poverty mind-set is due to the training we received in the Western seminaries built on Greek philosophies such as platonic dualism. Those philosophies teach about the dichotomy of light and darkness, the good and the bad; therefore, mixing up material things and spiritual things is unacceptable. The mind-set dictates that if we want to be spiritual, we are required to deny ourselves material things. Therefore, to love the Lord meant to deny oneself of worldly wealth and possessions.[14]

One good historical example is the third and fourth centuries after the apostles passed away. The entire monastic movement was soon created. Some gave away their riches and even came out of their married life to lead a simple or monastic life along the rivers or caves in order to achieve renewal and draw close to God. Some included well-known people such as Irenaeus of Lyons, Tertullian, Origen, and even St. Francis of Assisi.

In Asia, we have a double dilemma. Not only do we have to overcome the thought that prosperity is unacceptable for Christians but that for *full-time* Christian workers, it is a definite *no-no* to be seen as prosperous. To be seen as prosperous while serving God is controversial. This poverty mind-set is strongly entrenched in the church in Asia. Heavily influenced by the model of the Buddhist monastic movement in Asia, including those in China, the belief was that those serving in full-time ministries for God need to deny everything and have nothing to do with this world. To be spiritual meant the renouncing of wealth and riches. It is common that Christians take on cultural mind-sets such as poverty without thought of studying the culture of the kingdom of God.

Little wonder that many of us continue to think that in order to be spiritual, we must be poor. Biblically, we need to strike a balance—as Paul said, to "know how to be abased and to abound" (see Philippians 4:12). Learn how to be spiritual in times of need, and to be equally spiritual in times of plenty and prosperity.

Prosperity can come in several forms. There are four dimensions of prosperity:

+ physical (health);
+ spiritual (growing and maturing in the Lord);
+ social (your family being blessed by God and experiencing unity); and
+ material (wealth).

Many words about the transference of wealth have come forth. In early 2006, my church received a sum of 2.15 million Malaysian Ringgit, approximately $750,000 USD, from the Malaysian government as compensation for appropriating a portion of our land for a highway project.

> You shall remember the LORD your God, for it is He who gives you power to get wealth, that He may establish His covenant which He swore to your fathers, as it is this day.
> —DEUTERONOMY 8:18

> Command those who are rich in this present age not to be haughty, nor to trust in uncertain riches but in the living God, who gives us richly all things to enjoy. Let them do good, that they be rich in good works, ready to give, willing to share, storing up for themselves

a good foundation for the time to come, that they may lay hold on eternal life.

—1 TIMOTHY 6:17–19

In the New Testament, the church accepts the fact that there are rich people in the church. The Book of 1 Timothy acknowledges the rich and even lays out instructions about how to use their wealth.

6. LOCAL CHURCH MIND-SET VS. KINGDOM MIND-SET

During our current time in history, much emphasis is on the local church. Unfortunately, we have not seen the local church as an effective agent of change for the nations. Change is always scary and uncomfortable. However, as steps are taken toward change, we need to realize that our church is not the only church that God is going to use to change the nations. Other churches will be moved toward this new direction as well, according to their specific giftings and callings.

Previously I had a mind-set to guide our church into becoming a big church in numbers. That would be the only way to touch other nations. Subconsciously, most of us have been thinking that way, equating numbers with success in ministry. But after over thirty years and two major splits in my church, I cannot claim that the church has grown in numbers; nor can I say that it is anywhere near being the biggest church in the nation or the city. Then, I started to realize that our calling is not to be the biggest church in the land or the city. God has called us to be a pioneer of new ideas and revelation over the years.

When the church was pioneered in 1976, we were already moving in the apostolic ministry, and we managed to plant a few dozen churches within a short time. We were blessed with the prophetic gift, delivering prophetic words to individuals, prophesying over churches and ministries. The church was moving in a Davidic form of worship, where we danced unto the Lord and sang in the Spirit, more than thirty years ago while this was relatively new and unacceptable by other churches. We were viewed as strange people and out of this planet! However, as these gifts and moving in the Holy Spirit have become more accepted in churches nowadays, it has become the norm to be prophetic and to sing and dance unto the Lord. I say this not out of pride but out of a revelation of who we are and what we are supposed to be.

Several years ago I heard the Lord telling me to minister beyond the Latter Rain Church. Then Barbara Wentroble came and prophesied to my wife, Lily, to mentor men and women into the ministry, and that they will be not only in Latter Rain Church but also outside it. This was a major adjustment for us. I started by joining other spiritual fathers to gather together to pray for our nation. This resulted in the formation of the National Leaders Gathering, whose sole purpose was to bring leaders to pray together for the transformation of our beloved country, Malaysia. Then there was a major shift in Malaysia: as a result of the election, the opposition coalition parties were given five states, and the ruling national party lost their two-thirds majority in Parliament for the first time. This meant that the ruling national party could not pass any law pertaining to the national constitution as they would like, as that would require a two-thirds majority.

The leadership of Fullness of Christ International Ministries in Manila honored Lily and me by asking us to be its spiritual parents or advisors. Over several years we have seen growth in both numbers and the impact of this church in the city of Manila. We also have ordained their pastors and regularly visit them. Diwa Guinigundo, Deputy Governor of the Central Bank, the counterpart of the US Federal Reserve, is now senior pastor along with his wife, Apple.

In Singapore, Lily's former pastors began to develop a close relationship with us and looked to us as their mentors and spiritual advisors of their church. Strategic changes were taking place. The church moved from a maintenance church model into an apostolic church model.

In our travels in Australia, both in Melbourne and Gold Coast, we are also mentoring a number of pastors, businessmen, and a city councilor for nation transformation.

Today, God is speaking to us about moving toward nation transformation and linking with marketplace apostles. I do hope and expect many other churches to follow in the near future, although the idea doesn't seem to be popular right now with most people.

We can't do it alone. We need to network with the spiritual fathers in the nations, the apostles and prophets, as well as the marketplace men and women in all spheres of influence. Great transference of wealth and shifts in world and market systems will happen and bring change to nations. Our responsibility is to be prepared and work with like-minded men and women both in church-related ministry and in the marketplace.

7. NEGATIVE MIND-SET VS. POSITIVE MIND-SET

The negative thought says, *I cannot do it.* The positive thought says, *With God, I can do it.*

Personally, I was not good at studies. While in primary school, I failed miserably in my examinations. I was in a lower-ranked class and even repeated Standard 6 (grade 6, or the last year of primary school)! I never thought I could achieve anything in life and felt like a total failure. Then God changed my mind-set, and I became very successful in my studies.

While studying in Australia in 1974, I scored straight As besides doing two other external degrees. When I was at Fuller Theological Seminary in California, the dean of the School of World Mission, Paul Pierson, asked me if I could do my doctorate degree alongside my master's. Already finding the master's program rather overwhelming, I thought the task to be virtually impossible for me. But then God began to change my mind-set. They say that when we grow old, our gray matter starts to *rust.* It is not true! I did my studies for the master's degree while I was in my forties, and completed it before touching fifty. My grades improved greatly, and I scored almost all As.

Most Asians have exceptionally low self-esteem, especially the older generation. We were not taught to be competitive creatures. From our youth we were taught to share and give to others. Unfortunately, most parents thought that open praise would spoil their children and that criticism would mold their character. Subliminally, Asians traditionally have had this feeling that they are inferior and insignificant. In the past, even their songs were often played out in melancholic, minor keys, and were broken-hearted in nature! Both traditional and modern entertainment shows feature mother-in-law conflicts, people dying, hearts breaking. You will see it often in China, the Philippines, Thailand, and Malaysia. It is time we say, "With God, we can do it!" and break out of the old mold.

> A little one shall become a thousand, a small one a strong nation. I, the LORD, will hasten it in its time.
>
> —ISAIAH 60:22

I believe that this is the word of God for us at this time.

When Peter Wagner asked me to be the Coordinator for Spiritual Warfare in Southeast Asia in 1989, I declined. Peter then went to Cindy Jacobs and said, "Nobody ever said *no* to me, but Dexter did." After one year, he still hadn't found anybody. Cindy told Peter to talk to me again, and this time Peter wisely arranged to have lunch with Cindy Jacobs present.

Peter asked me again, "Will you take this job?"

I answered, "I won't mind if you need me to, but I don't think I'm the right guy."

Cindy quickly interjected, "Yes, you're the right guy."

I asked Cindy, "Are you very sure?"

"Yes, I'm very sure", she replied.

"If you're very sure, I'm OK with that," I responded.

On the way back from lunch, I was walking with Cindy, and I said to her, "Cindy, you've just given me lots of problems, did you know that? The devil will be after me now."

Sure enough, I have never experienced so many problems in my life! My wife, Lily, almost died due to a stroke; we had two church splits that drained me emotionally. I lost the strength and courage to raise up new generations for ministry. The fear of failure and rejection was so great. The desire to raise up new churches left me. For many years, I was afraid that a new set of people would again leave, and this caused me to think, *I am a failure*. However, I decided to change my negative mind-set to a positive one.

I went all out to develop the Southeast Asia Spiritual Warfare Network. I convened two significant meetings with Peter Wagner in Malaysia with delegates coming from Singapore, Thailand, Indonesia, Brunei, and as far as Cambodia and Myanmar. Then I traveled frequently to Indonesia, Thailand, and the Philippines to teach and speak at Prayer and Spiritual Warfare Conferences. In 1996 a large delegation from the Southeast Asian Region attended the World Evangelism Conference in Guatemala convened by Harold Caballeros, the Spiritual Warfare Network of Central America.

Peter Wagner commented when he was in Malaysia that only two regions in the world are active and very successful: one is Central America under the leadership of Harold Caballeros and the other is Southeast Asia under my leadership. That statement was enough to encourage me that my negative mind-set had turned into a positive one. I realized that by choice I had made a stand for what God had for me regardless of how inadequate I felt.

With regard to the churches and pastors that split away from us, I had to commit the situation to God. I poured out my heart to Him many times when I went through such painful experiences, and I told Him, "I surrender Latter Rain Churches into Your hands, Lord; they are Yours. If You want me to start all over again, I'll do it." I had to pick up from where we were and rise again, although when memories of happy and great times flooded my mind, there was emptiness in my heart. I was reminded of God's calling upon my life when I was nineteen years of age. He had awakened me from my sleep, given me a vision in the form of a very bright light, and spoken audibly to me for half an hour regarding my call. He said, "I knew you by name before the foundation of the world. I have given you gifts, and you shall preach My Word around the world."

Though I came from a poverty-stricken family, as my father was jobless for a number of years and I had to earn my own living since I was six years of age, those words brought tears to my eyes. I knew I was *a nobody*, but God had a great purpose for my life, and He knows me personally. That was in 1969.

Several years later, in 1972, a couple from the United States who are gifted with prophetic ministries prophesied to me similar words although we had never met. That took place in the home of our friends in Johor Bahru, a city in Malaysia close to Singapore. That was divine affirmation, and God opened doors for me to study in Singapore and Australia and then sent me home to Malaysia to pioneer Latter Rain Church. Currently we have some twenty churches both in East and West Malaysia. God confirmed our message with signs, wonders, and miracles.

In a God-appointed time in 2006, Chuck Pierce came with Peter Wagner to speak at the Apostolic Conference in Malaysia. In the afternoon meeting, Chuck called me out to the platform and prophesied and declared that God had given me a pair of red boxing gloves to fight the devil off from attacking my ministry. Suddenly, I felt the heaviness that had followed me lift. God also returned my son Elijah Low from the United States where he had studied and worked for some years. He assists me in the ministry. As a result of that prophetic word, no more church splits happened after 2002, and the work both consolidated and grew. Good growth is taking place among unreached people groups in Sarawak, formerly British Borneo. Currently we have an emphasis on growing the mother church in Kuala Lumpur into a city church that will be positioned as an agency for nation transformation. Kuala Lumpur is the federal capital and most populous in Malaysia.

The Lord sent Barbara Wentroble to us in the darkest moment of our lives when my wife, Lily, almost died of a stroke. When I had arrived home, her heart had stopped beating and her countenance was white as a sheet of paper. I had to call her spirit to come back to life.

Within a few days' time, we were on our way to attend the Gideon 300 meeting in Seoul, South Korea. After we arrived in South Korea, we were about to board a bus to Prayer Mountain when someone came down from the bus screaming, "Lily Low Malaysia!" We were shocked, but a persistent sister came forward and insisted she wanted to meet up with us again once we reached Prayer Mountain.

Once we arrived there, this lady introduced herself as an intercessor from Dallas. She revealed how God had burdened her to pray for Lily Low from Malaysia, especially on a particular day several days ago. She wanted to know if there was such a person, as she was praying for her. The Lord had told her to go to Seoul, South Korea, and she would find her. Because we arrived a day late, she could not locate Lily. But when she saw her name tag, she screamed. On the day that Lily had a stroke and was supposed to be dying, the intercessor had a tremendous burden to pray for Lily Low of Malaysia. She then introduced Lily to Barbara Wentroble, who ministered to her day and night for several days. She was gracious and kind in ministering to Lily, and the Lord used her to heal Lily from her trauma and deep hurts that she had suffered from the recent church split.

Barbara spoke completely accurate words of knowledge regarding what had happened to Lily, and Barbara knew by the Holy Spirit the words that had been spoken to hurt Lily. Lily recovered completely within a few months. Barbara has traveled to Malaysia to minister regularly. Since then, many other precious servants of God have given input into our lives and ministries and even our nation. Chuck Pierce, Barbara Yoder, Jim Hodges, and Hope Taylor are some of those who have strong links with us. It is a constant decision when you appeal before God to stand up again and again rather than to stay fallen.

With renewed mind-sets, we are now able to look at things from a fresh perspective and not be easily discouraged or feel defeated by the magnitude of the challenge. We also realize that a big portion of the church is out there in the marketplace and society. People who work in various government agencies, business, the media, education, and the arts and entertainment are those who are involved in marketplace ministries the same way as Daniel and Joseph were in the Old Testament. That is a specific calling, and they should be recognized by church leaders. God placed them in the marketplace to fulfill His purposes in order that these areas of influence can be brought into alignment with God's purposes. And we need thousands of them positioned in various areas of society. They need to be inspired with a renewed, positive mind-set to bring about changes for the better.

CHAPTER 4
INFLUENCING *the* MOLDERS *of* CULTURE

*I*N JOSHUA 14, Caleb had served God for forty years and was now eighty years old. Due to the unbelief of the Israelites, he and Joshua wandered in the wilderness for almost forty years before they finally entered the Promised Land. Joshua asked Caleb, "What do you want?" Caleb could have asked for the regions that were already conquered. After all, no one was more senior than him except Joshua.

Caleb said to Joshua:

> You know the word which the LORD said to Moses the man of God concerning you and me in Kadesh Barnea. I was forty years old when Moses the servant of the LORD sent me from Kadesh Barnea to spy out the land, and I brought back word to him as *it was* in my heart. Nevertheless my brethren who went up with me made the heart of the people melt, but I wholly followed the LORD my God. So Moses swore on that day, saying, "Surely the land where your foot has trodden shall be your inheritance and your children's forever, because you have wholly followed the LORD my God." And now, behold, the LORD has kept me alive, as He said, these forty-five years, ever since the LORD spoke this word to Moses while Israel wandered in the wilderness; and now, here I am this day, eighty-five years old. As yet I *am as* strong this day as on the day that Moses sent me; just as my strength *was* then, so now *is* my strength for war, both for going out and for coming in. Now therefore, give me this mountain of which the LORD spoke in that day; for you heard in that day how the Anakim *were* there, and *that* the cities *were* great *and* fortified. It may be that the LORD *will be* with me, and I shall be able to drive them out as the LORD said.
>
> —JOSHUA 14:6–12

THE SEVEN MOLDERS OF CULTURE

The concept of the seven spheres of influence is not new, as it has been around for years. Lance Wallnau, a business consultant, teaches frequently on what he calls the seven mountains. These seven molders or seven spheres of influence are the parameters to define nation transformation. Peter Wagner sometimes refers to them as the seven molders of culture.

This list of seven areas to be transformed was originally formulated by Loren Cunningham, founder of Youth With a Mission, and Bill Bright, founder of Campus Crusade for Christ. They were both leaders of the Lausanne Conference on World Evangelism in 1974. In 1975 when the two men met, they found that each had independently received revelation from God about the same seven areas that will cause the nations to turn to God and to shape society.[1] During that same time frame, Francis Schaeffer was given a similar message. In 1955 Schaeffer and his wife, Edith, founded The L'Abri communities, which are study centers in Europe, Asia, and America.

Basically, the message was that if we are to impact any nation for Jesus Christ, then we have to affect the seven spheres of influence, or mountains of society, that are the pillars of any society. Namely, these are:

+ Family
+ Religion
+ Government
+ Media
+ Education
+ Business
+ Arts and Entertainment

The spheres of influence in culture and nations are more than mere institutions in society. They have principalities and powers controlling them. We need to engage in spiritual warfare to dethrone their authority. The apostles and prophets should provide the leadership and make proclamations to break down the strongholds and powers of darkness. As God's church, we must rise up and function as His vehicle for nation transformation. Otherwise, some other forces will take the wheel and steer the direction of the nation off course toward evil and chaos. We need to carry out three crucial things:

+ Link up the church-based apostles with the marketplace apostles.
+ Network beyond our own churches.
+ Develop a coalition of the willing.

If we depend only on church-based ministries, only two out of the seven spheres of influence in culture will be impacted. Our churches can have great influence over two of the spheres—religion, and to a certain extent, families—but that is insufficient to create enough momentum to transform a nation. That explains why a nation like the Philippines, although a supposedly Christian nation, remains economically at the bottom of the ladder of emerging nations in Asia. Corruption is so entrenched in its government that the nation's wealth is not enjoyed by its people and nearly half of its population lives in poverty.

I can understand why many denominations, networks of churches, and independent churches care for their own and are charting their own courses. As founder and chairman of my own church movement, the Latter Rain Church of Malaysia, we did the same. Firstly, as an indigenous movement, we struggled much in pioneering our churches without asking for any financial support and missionaries from Western countries because we held on to the principle that Christianity is not a Western religion as perceived by non-Christians who are Buddhists, Hindus, and Muslims. Secondly, we believed our purpose was to focus on our vision, and that is to plant churches across our nations, even among unreached people groups in Sarawak, as well as developing leaders and ministries. Thirdly, we are involved in interdenominational organizations such as the National Evangelical Fellowship of Malaysia, Spiritual Warfare Network under the AD2000 and Beyond Movement, and numerous national interdenominational events. However, the Lord had to speak and instruct me to get involved in networking beyond my churches several years ago. Apparently the Lord had a different idea than I did.

The first time He spoke to me was during the National Convention of the Latter Rain Church in Cameron Highlands, Malaysia. Barbara Wentroble was able to gather a formidable team of ministers to join her in ministering to our network. The team members were Barbara Yoder, Chuck Pierce, and

Jim Hodges. This was the first time these team members ministered together in Asia. The ministry was powerful and greatly impacted everyone. During one of the meetings, I felt compelled to do identification repentance, as I felt convicted by the Lord to repent on behalf of many Asian leaders who disliked Western missionaries and as a result had not wanted to network with Western ministries and networks.

It was in the 1970s during my student days in Bible college in Singapore where we saw and judged wrongly. Our American missionaries were well paid, stayed in big bungalow houses, sent their children to expensive international schools, drove good cars, and had a good quality of life beyond the ordinary lifestyle in the country. Local pastors and workers like us were paid very meager incomes, about 10 percent to 20 percent of what the Western missionaries were paid, and that did not include vacations and other benefits. I have since learned that many of the missionaries had made great sacrifices in terms of having to forgo their lucrative careers as well as their families and friends. They also left their comfortable lifestyles and had to adjust to foreign cultures.

I had to repent before the team from the United States and ask them to forgive me, and I stood as a representative of many Asian pastors and leaders. I confessed that these missionaries from the West came and selflessly gave their lives, their families, and their all to share with us the gospel of Jesus Christ. As a result, a harvest of souls came to know Jesus Christ as Lord.

Of course, these four ministers of God graciously forgave us, and they came over to pray and release blessings on me and the rest of the Asian pastors and leaders. Chuck Pierce then asked for a belt and asked me to hold it tight while the four of them held on to the other end of the belt as a prophetic act. He proclaimed that God was binding our lives and network together. Several years later we joined FMCI, the Federation of Ministries and Churches International, which is led by Jim Hodges, and this has been a great blessing to me personally and to our network of churches as we forge ahead to see transformation of nations.

The second time the Lord spoke to me was in relation to my country, Malaysia. He asked me to network with pastors and leaders beyond my church network. That was hard because I understood by then that God wanted me to link my life and heart with like-minded pastors and leaders for the purpose of taking our place and authority as gatekeepers of our nation and to intercede corporately by coming together for a season. My greatest fear in these gatherings was that I would bump into my former pastors and leaders who had left me over the years. I would rather not turn up if I knew some of them would be there.

During the first Fathers Gathering, I met two couples that I had hoped would not be there, as I knew it would be hard for me to cope emotionally with unpleasant memories flashing through my mind. I did try to behave as graciously as I could to these two couples besides trying to relate with many others. Then came the last day, when Communion was served. One of the couples came over to ask for forgiveness, and over a good amount of tears, we prayed, and my wife and I released generational blessings on them and forgave them for pulling their church away from our network. Since then, these two couples have become close to us again. Since we prayed, whenever we have met, the fellowship has been sweet and precious.

Many more who had left us came back to restore our relationship, and this gave us much joy. It is the knitting of hearts that is significant before God. Only then can we pray, agree, and decree together in the heavenlies with great results. However, in gathering leaders together, those who join are those pastors of smaller churches and independent churches. Several pastors from denominational churches may join from time to time, but pastors of megachurches of several thousand members will rarely gather together.

Unfortunately, many leaders of large churches cannot see this picture. I find this happening in many nations during my travels. Therefore, let us start first with the coalition of the willing. Those who are willing, let them work together first. One day we hope that perhaps some of the elephants will join us. For now, we may look more like a team of mouse-deer, cats and dogs—but God can still work something through us. We have to start somewhere, and we must not be discouraged, for this is a long haul. Some may drop, but others may join. What is important is to keep up the pace and momentum and see tangible changes begin to take place as we walk and pray corporately.

> Who hath despised the day of small things? for they shall rejoice, and shall see the plummet in the hand of Zerubbabel with those seven; they are the eyes of the LORD, which run to and fro through the whole earth.
> —ZECHARIAH 4:10, KJV

THE FIRST SPHERE OF INFLUENCE: RELIGION

Religion that includes the church is one of the first spheres of influence in culture. Three important criteria must be examined before we can accomplish this.

1. Prepare for a great harvest of souls.

In Malaysia a great harvest is awaiting to be reaped among those who do not know Christ. According to the 2014 CIA World Factbook, as of July 2014 the population of Malaysia was 30,073,353, ranking no. 44 in the world.[2] The population of Christians in Malaysia is 9.2 percent,[3] and only a little over 2,760,000.[4] There is much work to be done.

2. Understand that the church is not just about getting souls saved but also about planting strong churches with a nation transformation mandate.

The church in each nation must be trained and have a vision regarding its God-given mandate as an agency of nation transformation.

In Sarawak, 42.6 percent of the population of two million people may be Christians, according to governmental statistics based on the year 2010; however, most Christian leaders would agree that more than half of the population are Christians, but they appear powerless to influence society. They do not seem to make much difference or impact. Also, the government in Malaysia is Muslim, so it suppresses minority religions. A number are in positions of government leadership in the state and several at the federal level. We do not see a significant kingdom influence representing the Christians who reside in the State of Sarawak.

3. Ask for revival among God's people.

Those who are dormant, apathetic, and have lost their fire need revival. Many are returning to their old ways and lifestyles. They need to recover their passion and fervent love for God again. The church must pray for revival so that God will bring down His fire and redeem lives for His purposes again.

Revival, signs and wonders, miracles, and conversions! These occurrences can change and shift the spiritual atmosphere of a region. Look at Almolonga, Guatemala, for example. As more people received Christ in their lives, even the physical land was redeemed. Our cry is for God to forgive our sins and heal our land (2 Chron. 7:14). Fertile land can become productive land, abundant with minerals, gold, and riches.

In Malaysia, John Sung brought revival among those who spoke Foo Chow, a Chinese dialect, especially in Sitiawan town in West Malaysia and in the State of Sarawak in the 1930s, which resulted in spectacular growth of the Chinese Methodist Church in these places.

At the same time in 1930s, the Lun Bawang tribe on the mountain of Ba'Kelalan in the State of Sarawak, East Malaysia, experienced the first wave of revival. However, it was the Bario Revival of 1973, which took place in the mountainous northeastern region of Sarawak among the Kelabit tribe, that was significant. The revival began among students and later spread among SIB (Sidang Injil Borneo) denomination, the indigenous church movement pioneered by the BEM (Borneo Evangelical Mission) that resulted in evangelism and church planting. Moreover, "Bill Hawes categorically singled out the Bario Revival as the most significant factor in the development of the established churches in Sarawak during the period from 1973 to 1976."[5] The Bario Revival not only changed the people but notably advanced God's kingdom in several ways, including their social life and culture.

According to Penghulu Ngimat Ayu, the tribal chief in Kelabit Highlands, he had hardly any dispute to settle between 1973 and 1976 because the parties concerned had decided to forgive one another. There were no reports of theft, as stolen properties were returned or compensated for in some way.

The community transformation affected the children immensely, resulting in them being more responsible. Between 1972 and 1976 the Bario Secondary School maintained one of the highest passing rates in the Sarawak Junior Certificate Examination. Though limited in resources, many of these students advanced their studies in the universities and became very successful professionals. Between 1979 and 1982, we had the privilege of hosting several of these students who were touched and used by the Lord in our home while they were studying in the university. We shared with them what little we had and loved them as our own while we pioneered a new church in the neighborhood of the university near the city.

In 2001, though Bario had only a few thousand inhabitants, it was picked as one of the top seven most intelligent communities in the world as announced in New York on August 10, 2001, by the World Teleport Association website (www.worldteleport.org). WTA is the world's only international trade association for teleports and their development partners. WTA's Intelligent Community Forum within the association focuses on the uses of broadband technology for economic development by communities large and small in both the developed and developing world. The top seven communities selected were Bario, Malaysia; Ennis, Ireland; LaGrange, Georgia (USA); Nevada, Missouri (USA); New York City, New York (USA); Singapore; and Sunderland, England.[6]

Here is the citation:

> An atypical community for an award usually associated with high-tech corridors such as Malaysia's own Multimedia Supercorridor, Bario, is located in the remotest highlands of Borneo, Malaysia. Although Bario residents, known as the Kelabits, are without phones or public electricity, its elders learned from researches at the Malaysian University of Sarawak the benefits of being connected to the world via the internet. The researchers received a grant from both the Malaysian and Canadian governments to determine how the people of Bario would use technology for sustainable social development. Through satellite connectivity provided by Telekom Malaysia Bhd, computer courses have started in the school and a telecenter, a modest house with PCs, scanners and a terminal and have been established to allow the residents to perform a range of online functions related to economic development. To date it is an initiative to network with local agriculture authorities to boost outside sales of Bario's special form of rice, which is renowned throughout the country for its sweet fragrance.[7]

The Bario community was also awarded in March 6, 2002, the 2002 Industry Innovators Award winners in New York given by the Society of Satellite Professionals International (SSPI) in recognition of organizations in both the for-profit and nonprofit sectors that had made outstanding contributions to the development and growth of the global satellite industry.

The other significant revival took place in the mid-1980s among the Lun Bawangs. They are considered linguistically as first cousins of the Kelabits. This time God manifested Himself in Ba'Kelalan in signs and wonders including a spectacular display of light in the heavens that appeared over a series of nights, and miracles of some rice and little water turning to flour, cooking oil, and sugar enough to bake traditional rice cakes to feed two hundred people who were present, and with plenty leftovers. These signs, wonders, and miracles were recorded according to their chronological occurrences and edited by Ariel Chew in the unpublished paper, "The Sign/Wonder/Miracles in Ba'Kelalan 1984–1986."[8]

In March 2011 we sent a team of three people to visit Ba'Kelalan to stay and participate in various church activities. Recently, some of their leaders visited us, and we discovered that God has raised their entire community as prayer warriors and intercessors for the nation. Their primary school equivalent to Junior Certificate Level is currently the best performing school in the whole district. Their land is so fertile that they have a bumper harvest for their crops, and they are the only place to grow apples. They are praying that a highway or a good roadway be built to connect their highlands to other towns and cities to enable them to transport and sell their many farm products. This is an important infrastructure that they have lacked.

Their children are as successful as the Kelabits, furthering their studies in various institutions of higher learning and universities. This community has been so transformed that when guests and government officials visit their community, they welcome them with singing hymns and worship songs. Their prayers and intercession cover many hours on Sundays, and after worship service everyone in the community stays for community lunch.

The religion sphere of culture must be conquered. People must come to the Lord, and multitudes will receive salvation. Apostles, prophets, and intercessors need to link up in one heart to see revival and signs and wonders breaking forth.

If we don't move quickly to evangelize, some false religion will. The ungodly will continue to rule. At the same time we must ensure that the churches are revived and renewed, so that they will have the power and influence to touch the lives of people around them. When the church becomes nominal and cold, it cannot be effective and loses its relevance to the world and society at large.

But influencing culture with religion alone cannot transform a nation. Six other spheres of influence are waiting to be conquered.

THE SECOND SPHERE OF INFLUENCE: FAMILY

The second sphere of influence in culture is the family, one of God's vital institutions in society. If you look at the Philippines, thousands of families are without mothers because the mothers have gone all over the world, employed as contract workers to earn a better living for their families. What happens to their husbands? Many of them begin having extramarital affairs, even taking another wife. Most of the children grow up to become rebellious and disobedient. They gain the money but lose the family.

According to UNICEF, "the Philippines is the major supplier of labor migrants to over one hundred countries and the leading female migrant sending countries along with Indonesia. More than eight million (10 percent) of the 85 million Filipinos were working or living abroad...over 72 percent of total migrants from Philippines were women workers. Many of these women work as domestic helpers, nurses, caregivers, and entertainers. With this huge number of Filipino migrants (and still more) [leaving] the country temporarily (or permanently), a more pressing concern is with regards to children left behind. Though there is no systematic data on the number of children left behind, it is estimated to be nine million or 27 percent of the total youth."[9]

The enemy's plan is to break up families and bring division and divorce. If you lose the family, how can God's blessings flow from one generation to the next? When the hearts of the fathers are not turned to the children, and the children's hearts are not turned to the fathers, God says He will bring a curse upon the nation. How can the nation be blessed and prosper if this curse is upon it? This is where apostles, prophets, and intercessors need to work together and bring forth transformation to redeem families. Through acts of identification repentance, they can pray on behalf of families and generations. Only then can reconciliation and healing take place.

I remember vividly the Establishing the Prophetic Destiny of the Philippines Conference in San Juan Arena in Quezon City, Manila, where some six thousand participants were present including pastors, congressmen, and a congresswoman. I asked by a show of hands how many of them had experienced having fathers or mothers being sent to other countries as contract workers and had been deprived of their father's or mother's love and presence. At least 80 percent raised their hands. As I thought they did not understand my question, I repeated my question but received the same result. I asked whether this was true, and the Filipino leaders and pastors sitting at the front portion nodded their heads in affirmation. I was overwhelmed. Because of their sheer numbers, it was not possible for all to come forward, so I asked them to stand.

I told them we should do identification repentance. I asked the mothers and fathers to stand and take the place of participants who grew up without a mother or father to be with them, leaving emptiness in their hearts. These fathers and mothers would approach those who raised their hands. Then I asked the important question, "On behalf of your fathers and mothers, would you forgive me for leaving you and going away overseas to work for many years, causing you to grow up with emptiness in your hearts without the presence and love of your father or mother?" I instructed those who represented mothers and fathers to ask these who stood up and raised their hands, "On behalf of your mum and dad, would you forgive me?" These participants needed to answer, "Yes, I forgive you, Mom or Dad."

On the other hand, these sons and daughters who suffered also needed to ask forgiveness from their fathers and mothers for the sacrifice that they made to earn money in order to send their children to good schools and higher institutions of learning. Now the sons and daughters had their turn to ask for forgiveness by saying, "Mom, Dad, would you forgive me for having unforgiveness in my heart toward you and not appreciating the sacrifice you made for me by working overseas to earn enough to pay for my education so that I would be successful and not suffer in poverty like you?" Those standing in for fathers and mothers would say, "I forgive you."

There was not a dry eye there in that meeting as tears flowed freely with loud sobbing. Then I had to proclaim, "Lord, let Your healing flow, and bind the hearts of fathers and mothers with their sons and daughters." That is the way for reconciliation to take place and for families to be healed and united. Only then can generational blessings flow from fathers to sons. When three generations can be connected together, there will be the release of the power of synergy, where greater things can be accomplished and greater vision can be fulfilled as they work together.

The challenge now is for the church to raise up wholesome families, and provide good models of strong marriages and healthy, godly families. More and more marriages are breaking up. Recently, through spending time with a Christian lawyer in the Gold Coast, Australia, I was shocked to learn that 50 percent of her divorce cases involve Christians. Marriages are breaking up even among churchgoers. Sadly, it seems to be an accepted trend. Churches seem to be apathetic and indifferent to divorces in the Western world, as if it is the norm. At least one in two marriages in Western countries ends up in divorce.

Families are the foundational building block of a nation, so if marriages and families are broken up, it has adverse effects upon the nation. This is why the devil is attacking families and the institution of marriage. Divorce leads to a fatherless and motherless generation who will rise up to be rebellious against God. God wants to see sons and daughters being fathered, but the devil tries to destroy relationships between fathers and sons.

Prevention is better than cure

Do we want to raise up children who are emotionally marred and rebellious because of broken homes? Prevention is always better than cure. Unfortunately, most Christian ministries in these nations tend to focus more on remedial ministries for single parents, street kids, abandoned kids, and so forth, while break-ups in marriages and homes are spiraling into alarming figures. We are dealing with the effects rather than the cause! We should be trying to raise up more wholesome and godly families and marriages. We need to pray that families bring up children in the ways of God.

> This is why the devil is attacking families and the institution of marriage. Divorce leads to a fatherless and motherless generation who will rise up to be rebellious against God. God wants to see sons and daughters being fathered, but the devil will try to destroy that relationship between fathers and sons.

Issues like gay rights are gaining momentum in the Western world, especially in America. Being homosexual is suddenly acceptable. The term "gay" has become popular, as it referred to feelings of happy, carefree or bright and showy, but it is only a cover-up for the true results of living a homosexual lifestyle. Even one or two cases of gay pastors have surfaced in Malaysia. The whole aim is to attack the institution of marriage.

The question is this: *Who has more influence over families? The church or the world?* Unfortunately, in our time, it appears that the media has more influence than the church. In Australia, many television programs are filled with immoral values and principles. Is it any wonder that children begin to adopt values such as premarital sex, adulterous relationships, marriage breakups, divorces, and single parenthood? Abortion is also an issue that is destroying families. Something is wrong about the general outlook of today's society. In other parts of the world, the situation is not much different. The wrong values and behavior are imparted by movies and TV programs that continue to influence and shape the next generation's values for the future.

Do we stand back and watch our moral values continue to decay for our children?

THE THIRD SPHERE OF INFLUENCE: GOVERNMENT

The government consists of three main components: the judiciary, legislative, and executive branches. We need to pray for those in all three branches of government, that they may serve the people with uprightness.

The judiciary branch

The judiciary branch includes the courts and judges. Judges uphold justice and righteousness in the land. An outcry is going on in Malaysia. The people's confidence in the judges of this nation is being shaken. This cry for justice is not just happening in Malaysia but is also occurring in other parts of the world, such as United States of America, Australia, and Pakistan.

The legislative branch

People need to be encouraged to move in these areas, to study law and take it up as a profession. Legislators, including state assemblymen and members of parliament, determine the direction of laws in the country. Laws that are oppressive and unjust should be improved, but this can only be done when the right people are in place.

The executive branch

Under the executive branch is the cabinet, state government, and local civil authorities such as mayors, city councilors, and village heads. We can be involved in all these areas and encourage many others to do so, be it in a leading or supportive role.

Other government agencies such as the police, army, and the Central Bank influence the nation's security and stability. For example, if power-hungry people control the army, they can overthrow governments, as we have seen in the past in countries like Thailand, Burma, and Fiji.

Engaging with the government

We can speak out as a prophetic voice to the government, or those walking in the corridors of power, when they go astray from what is righteous, just, and true. At the same time, we should be partnering with the government for nation-building, eliminating corruption and poverty. Generally, most government leaders and politicians see the church as an organization that is always out to get favors from the government, especially financial assistance. No, we are not going to them just for handouts. Our responsibility is to help them do a better job, pray for them, and help and support them in practical ways. We need members of parliament, regardless of what party they represent, to stand on God's side and uphold truth and righteousness for the nation.

Rather than political, we should be governmental. We are not siding with certain political parties, but we want to encourage each and every one in politics to stand for God and His principles. The question is not whose party God is joining, but, "Who is on God's side?" As responsible stewards of the kingdom of God, we should do thorough research on political candidates. Are they willing to make their stand clear on certain core issues? The Old Testament prophets functioned as God's mouthpieces to governments about righteousness and justice. They were fearless in speaking the word of God and were not afraid to offend. Those who listened to those prophetic words released God's blessings, but for those who did not listen, judgment came upon them.

In 1 Kings 21, Elijah prophesied concerning the judgment of God on Ahab after he wrongfully accused Naboth of cursing God and the king and then possessed his property as orchestrated by Jezebel, his wife. "In the place where dogs licked up Naboth's blood, dogs will lick up your blood—yes, yours!" (1 Kings 21:19, NIV). The judgment of God concerning Jezebel was no better: "Dogs will devour Jezebel by the wall of Jezreel" (1 Kings 21:23, NIV). The word of God concerning Ahab came to pass in 1 Kings 22:37–38: "So the king died…and the dogs licked up his blood, as the word of the LORD had declared."

Elijah prophesied about Jezebel:

> On the plot of ground at Jezreel dogs will devour Jezebel's flesh. Jezebel's body will be like refuse on the ground in the plot at Jezreel, so that no one will be able to say, "This is Jezebel."
>
> —2 KINGS 9:36–37, NIV

Just like relationships, engaging with the government is built on trust. In Gold Coast, I had the opportunity to minister to one of the city councilors who was sued for defamation. He was a whistleblower who revealed corruption by one of the top officials. I brought businesspeople together to pray for him, stand by him and surround him, and encourage him in his endeavor. Another lady councilor was sued for breaking local council law with regards to confidentiality by exposing a sex predator among the senior officials of the city council.

We need to stand by such people if we want to have a clean government. We need to pray for them, support them, and commission them in their roles, for that is God's calling for them. We must recognize that they are there by assignment from God. Like a two-edged sword, we can be used by God to deliver His prophetic words at the right time to key individuals and to make a stand against injustice and unrighteousness. That is our prophetic role as the church, the body of Christ.

THE FOURTH SPHERE OF INFLUENCE: BUSINESS

Business covers many different areas: entrepreneurship, banking, service industry, hotels, tourism, information and communication technologies, medical services, and all other commercial sectors. We need to see God's blessings come upon the business sector. For Christians in the business and professional community, their role is to make money. That is their ministry. There is nothing wrong with making big money as long as the source and means are clean. Money means influence and the ability to make things happen. Everybody knows that, even the government.

If you are not doing well, nobody will be listening to you. If you want to cause change in the country, become a successful businessperson with integrity who is able to make money. Then when you talk, the government will listen. The businesspeople have to start believing God for great transference of wealth to take place. So, it is about time that millionaires and businesspeople are raised up for God to exert the right kind of influence over governments and systems.

> God gives wisdom and knowledge and joy to a man who is good in His sight; but to the sinner He gives the work of gathering and collecting, that he may give to him who is good before God. This also is vanity and grasping for the wind.
> —ECCLESIASTES 2:26

The "good before God" are those who have been cleansed with the blood of the Lamb, and to these God has given wisdom, knowledge, and joy. But to the sinner God has given the commission to gather and collect in order to transfer the wealth to those who are good. Transference of wealth will take place in a big way when there is a shaking and shifts taking place in the economic realm. During an economic downturn or a financial crisis, things may suddenly sell for inexpensive prices. If you are ready and in a position to buy companies and properties at rock-bottom prices, transfer of wealth can take place very rapidly. When shaking takes place, both in the political and economic realm, we need to be alert and on the watch, moving into intercession as well as preparing to take action in the natural.

We need to pray that the business community will unlock the wealth of the nations, and begin bringing finances and resources for God's purposes and to empower the poor. Most important of all, pray that God's people will be good stewards of their time, talent, and resources. Let us not forget that God's purpose for transference of wealth is for nation transformation and eradication of poverty.

THE FIFTH SPHERE OF INFLUENCE: EDUCATION

We have many people involved in education in churches ranging from child-care and school teachers, principals, school administrators, education board officials, and university lecturers. These are people who have a big role in shaping the minds of the future generation.

Education is an area where future generations can be influenced to do great things for God at a time when young minds are the most impressionable. However, it can also swing to the other extreme. For instance, did you know that all the seeds of extremism, militancy, and terrorism are being sown in certain kindergartens? Even our own Malaysian government released a white paper stating that there are 50,000 enrolled in kindergarten classes in our country. In these places, sometimes the children are taught to be anti-government, militant and extremist in thinking. The government had no choice but to withdraw financial support or to close them down. Otherwise, they might risk raising a whole generation of extremists.

On the other hand, if we position ourselves in educational institutions, we can affect the destinies and shape the mind-sets of the young generation. Having the right people in strategic positions will enable them to make policy changes to affect education and touch the lives of many people.

Pray for freedom of education for all; the freedom to pursue knowledge and wisdom, and to educate the next generation with truth and knowledge. Ungodly curriculum and ideas need to be taken out. Continuously pray for those who are involved and have influence in the sphere of education that God will grant them freedom to think for the good of the nation.

The church should respond rapidly in this area to provide good education. Currently, many people are not happy with the education system of our nation, Malaysia. Let us pray that our education curriculum be more academic than religious and that the quality of teachers be improved rather than deteriorated.

In 2010 the Board of Education in the state of Texas approved a social studies curriculum putting a conservative stamp on history and economics textbooks that will stress the superiority of American capitalism, "questioning the Founding Fathers' commitment to a purely secular government and presenting Republican political philosophies in a more positive light...board members [had] been locked in an ideological battle between a bloc of conservatives who question Darwin's theory of evolution and believe the Founding Fathers were guided by Christian principles."[10]

The state is one of the largest buyers of textbooks. The final vote was ten to five to revise the liberal standards. According to a 2010 article:

> The new standards will be written next year [2012] and remain in effect for ten years. They will determine what the state's 4.8 million K–12 students are taught in government, world history, US history, and economics classes from kindergarten through high school. They will also be used to develop state tests and write textbooks. Significant media attention has been devoted to the state's debate over social studies guidelines because decisions made there have national impact. Since Texas is the largest single purchaser of textbooks, publishers tailor them to its guidelines. Typically more than 90 percent of America's textbooks are based on Lone Star State curriculum, as it is too costly to produce multiple versions.[11]

A popular concept adopted by many states is the Common Core standard. In 2013, the Texas Legislature passed a law prohibiting school districts from using Common Core in their lesson plans. Current Texas Governor Greg Abbott stands firmly against the Common Core.[12]

Inspiring innovation through education

Can we motivate and inspire young men and women to go into research, medicine, or biotechnology, to find new cures for cancer, diabetes, and so forth? Can we encourage our children and young people to engage in IT research as a way of bridging the gap between the developed nations and developing nations? We can move ahead of these developed nations in breaking new ground on IT innovation.

Biotechnology is gaining importance around the world because it is a billion-dollar industry for medicine. In our own backyard in Malaysia, we have a wealth of herbs and possible alternative medicine that is yet to be researched and developed for anti-aging, life longevity, general health, and even incurable diseases. We must encourage our young scientists to aim for the highest and break new ground. If God gives us wisdom and creativity, surely God can enable godly young scientists to discover new cures.

The Sixth Sphere of Influence: Arts and Entertainment

The young generation in the Western world has grown up with an MTV, McDonald's, rap, hip-hop, and video games culture. Within their blood is a love for dance, music, and performing arts. We are losing the young generation to MTV. They love MTV more than our worship music. Unfortunately, most churches are not offering the right opportunities for that generation.

We must reclaim from the devil what rightfully belongs to God. If we do not have any influence in the arts and entertainment circles, the whole generation of young people will be influenced by music and dance from other sources promoting the wrong values. At the same time, many famous artists who promote ungodly values and morals become their icons and role models. Let us start relating to this generation and learn to understand their interests. Provide good quality music and dance alternatives that they can identify with. Don't expect them to conform to yesterday's popular fads.

You lose the arts, you lose the youth. We need to redeem the arts and entertainment for God.

Music and dance are close to the heart of God. They flow from God and His very being. But churches in general seem to be out of touch and lagging behind in this area. Therefore, what choice do our young people have in terms of the sources of music, dance, and performing arts? You lose the arts, you lose the youth. We need to redeem the arts and entertainment for God so that we can have much to offer to the young generation.

God can raise up a new generation of young people who can compose Christian music and dance that appeal to their generation. We need to pray that the performing arts will reshape culture with godly values and that God will unleash creative power upon His people that they may present God in beauty, holiness, strength, and glory.

Carrie Underwood, the 2005 *American Idol* winner, sold more than a million copies of her song "Jesus, Take the Wheel" and was at the top of the American chart for six consecutive weeks. This song touched many lives around the world through its message of asking Jesus to take charge of our lives, and was especially popular among the young people. During the *American Idol* finale in 2008, which was watched by millions worldwide, the finalists chose to sing "Shout to the Lord."

Sherwood Baptist Church produced the movie *Fireproof* in 2008, which saved and restored many marriages. The church also touched many more lives through another movie, *Facing the Giants. Facing the Giants*, produced in 2006, had a small budget of $100,000. The film ultimately was shown in over 1,000 theaters and grossed a total of $10,178,331.[13] *Fireproof* was the number four independent film and the highest grossing independent film of 2008.[14] Who would expect that this church with a small budget could produce such quality firms with good Christian values that would be successful and influence many lives?

THE SEVENTH SPHERE OF INFLUENCE: MEDIA

TV, movies or cinema, radio, newspapers, and the Internet all play a very important role in nation transformation. Cindy Jacobs once gave me a prophetic word that I would appear on television. During one of my recent trips to the Philippines, it actually happened! I was invited to speak over television about nation transformation, and that program was aired through nationwide channels.

Media enables us to reach the masses. It also lends much credibility. Through the media, we can greatly influence the mind-sets of people. Unfortunately, the media is full of negative images and values nowadays.

The influence of media on the culture and its ability to mold minds are more than most realize. The media can either build you up or tear you down. If God's people have no influence over the media, the messages that affect the mind-set of the people will never glorify His name. The day will come when there will be Christian programs aired on TV and radio, even in nations like Malaysia that have banned Christian media. With freedom all over the world, we can show the world how great our God is, rather than being fed a media diet of all the negativity and falsehood.

An example of the media influencing the direction of a nation is the Canadian experience. The fathers of the nation used media well to expedite their mission. Suddenly, the entire nation began to be aware of spiritual leaders and the fathers of the nation coming together for this session of prayer, to humble themselves and work together for nation transformation. Wouldn't it be great to have godly people on the staff and the board of directors of these media outlets, so that they could advocate the dissemination of positive and better influence to the readers rather than focusing on negative reporting to boost their sales? It could also be a means of exposing injustice and corruption. At the same time, those who speak up for truth and justice could also be accurately publicized.

We need to pray that the media will communicate truth and have the courage and strength to defend the truth.

The Australians tell me how they need to shield their children from watching their local television productions because they are filled with immoral, ungodly values. During a visit to Gold Coast, Australia, I met a businessman from the Sunshine Coast. While I challenged those present to get businesspeople to buy at least one television channel in Australia, he was challenged. Why complain about all the bad values that are propagated through the shows? Why don't the businesspeople buy one studio or television channel, or at least become major shareholders, so that the policies of the company can be influenced for the better?

When my host rang him up a few days later, the businessman said that the personal meeting I had with him was important, as he was also having the same thing in mind. That word that I spoke to him was a confirmation that he should buy a television station, or at least be a substantial stakeholder. This same man is a remarkable person and was part of the Christian lobby that organized a television interview between the prime minister and the opposition leader at that time. God raised him up for the marketplace in a very special way.

This man grew up in South Africa with a violent military background, having joined the antiterrorist squad in Zimbabwe and risen to the top ranks. But he had an experience with God in Australia, and today he has started many businesses in that nation, from buildings to unit trusts. His aim is to be able to influence the government for God's purposes.

In the Philippines, broadcasting Christian programs over television is allowed. Let us pray that the time will come when we can also be free to broadcast and publish what is pleasing to God in Malaysia and other nations.

THE CHALLENGE: WHICH SPHERE OF
INFLUENCE DO YOU WANT TO PURSUE?

Caleb said, "Give me this mountain." He then conquered Hebron, where the sons of Anakim had lived. They were the giants, yet he conquered their whole generation. He said, "I do not need the whole twelve tribes. I and my father's house and my family are enough. I do not need the unbelievers to come and join me. I can conquer the mountain." And Caleb conquered the mountain in his time and generation. (See Joshua 14.)

God's people need to have the same desires as Joshua and Caleb, and say to God, "Give me this mountain." Our attitude should be that this is something worth giving our lives for—to see nations transformed for God's purposes, nation after nation. God's people can discover new business and economic models; find a cure for cancer; discover oil, gold, and resources, a new biodiesel, or even a new source of energy. He created us after His own image, and our nature is to create, just like Him. Sharpen up your prophetic skills and biblical knowledge, for God can use us in tremendous ways beyond our imaginations.

There may be giants, yes—plenty of them! However, as God's people, if the apostles, prophets, and intercessors begin to work together, we can break these powers of darkness. We can take these spheres of influence or molders of culture. But we need to arise and say, "Give me this mountain, in my time and my generation. Give it to me!" We missed it when we had the opportunity. Let us not miss it again in our time and generation.

Which of these seven mountains is God moving your heart for? There are many subdivisions under these seven spheres of influence. Identify where your place and calling is among them.

How do you want to influence the culture and mold the minds in the future generation? Which do you want God to give to you? With God at your side, you can do it!

CHAPTER 5
SPIRITUAL WARFARE:
KEYS *to* TRANSFORMING *a* NATION

*I*N THE YEAR 2005, I sensed the Lord speaking to me about transforming nations and fulfilling His destiny for the nations. There are a few keys that God has put upon my heart in order to see nations being transformed. I strongly feel that these keys are essential to unlocking the door for each nation to fully enter into its respective destiny.

1. REMOVE THE CURSE OF THE FATHERLESS

The first key to nation transformation is to remove the curse of the fatherless.

> Behold, I will send you Elijah the prophet before the coming of the great and dreadful day of the LORD. And he will turn the hearts of the fathers to the children, and the hearts of the children to their fathers, lest I come and strike the earth with a curse.
> —MALACHI 4:5–6

This speaks of the curse of the fatherless or the curse of being an orphan. It also includes the curse of broken relationships from one generation into the next. The link between the generations must take place, and I have already seen God doing it even in our midst. Part of this will be the restoration of fathers to father the orphans. God does not want us to be spiritual orphans anymore. He is raising up fathers with a true father's heart who will be willing to raise up spiritual children to achieve their highest potential. Once they begin believing God for their calling to be realized, they will be very successful people.

God wants unity within the family, with parents mentoring and guiding their children with excellence. The devil strategically seeks to destroy the family unit because it is the foundation of a healthy society. How many incidences have we heard about where broken families and children are scarred for life because of the mistakes of their parents? When families break up, the generational blessings and heritage cease to flow. It is a pity to see later generations lose out on the inheritance of their blessings. Our families are to be living testimonies of unity between the generations. This must take place before we can see the nations transformed.

2. REMOVE STRONGHOLDS

The next important key is to remove strongholds. They can affect us spiritually, emotionally, mentally, and physically. Sometimes these strongholds can also hinder financial blessings. There are several ways to remove these strongholds.

What are strongholds?

In 2 Corinthians 10:4–5 the Apostle Paul says, "For the weapons of our warfare are not carnal but mighty in God for pulling down strongholds, casting down arguments and every high thing that exalts itself against the knowledge of God, bringing every thought into captivity to the obedience of Christ." This means that "strongholds" can take on two different forms: "arguments" (Greek *logismos*) and "high things" (Greek *hupsoma*).

+ "Arguments" have to do with mind-sets of an individual; community; people group, such as American Indians, African Americans; or even a nation. Arguments are strongholds "rooted in human mind-sets or decisions or choices, whether by individuals or by groups such as national governments."[1] Therefore, when the United States government chose to break several hundred solemn treaties previously signed with the Native Americans, it caused a stronghold to be created among the Native Americans' mind-set and culture that can be used by Satan until it is pulled down. The pain and wounds of broken treaties and covenants are carried down through the generations unless repentance takes place.

Everywhere you go, you will find people who are full of negative mind-sets and heavily oppressed by failure and poverty. The failure and poverty mentality among people in the Philippines, Africa, and many other third-world countries[2] is a stronghold over their lives. Many of these people cannot believe that God can set them free from poverty. We have to overcome the mind-set of fear, intimidation, and failure that stops the people from trying, hoping, and daring to aim for success.

Sometimes these come as a result of generational curses. Sins of idolatry committed by our forefathers can result in a curse coming to the succeeding generations. Exodus 20:3–4 states clearly God's commandment not to worship other gods or make carved images and worship them as gods. For those who do so, God will visit "the iniquity of the fathers upon the children to the third and fourth generations" (Exod. 20:5). Negative mind-sets have also come to nations that were colonized by other nations in the past. This often tends to develop into a slave mentality. In the case of African Americans and Haitians, their root was slavery.

> • "High things" are spiritual principalities such as territorial spirits, demonic powers worshipped by the people, and the spiritual powers behind spirit mediums, all of which come from the demonic realm. Thus, to pull down such strongholds we need to use not carnal or human weapons but spiritual weapons that God has given us.

Through healing of past trauma, hurts, and generational curses

Cindy Jacobs must be credited for sharing with us that we must treat nations and people as individual persons. Just as an individual needs healing from hurts and trauma, so do nations.[3] Wounds that come as a result of past trauma and hurt allow the devil to build strongholds in our mind-set and hold the people captive. They can handicap us in our ministries, careers, and relationships. In a similar way, communities, people groups, and nations with untreated wounds and trauma caused by being colonized, conquered, defeated, or sold into slavery could become strongholds for the enemy to demoralize and hinder our progress.

In my association as one of the founding members of the International Spiritual Warfare Network, and since I was appointed coordinator of Southeast Asia under the leadership of Peter Wagner in 1989, I have witnessed firsthand numerous instances where healing over people groups and nations were taking place.

Apostolic and prophetic leaders working together with intercessors can be God's instruments to bring healing of the past wounds by standing in for their nations that oppressed such nations.

Cindy Jacobs related to my wife and me how the Lord had been sending her to countries that were colonized by the United States or hurt by CIA covert operations in undermining their governments in the past. Cindy's list included countries in Central America and the Philippines. She would stand in the gap as an intercessor, doing identification repentance on behalf of United States, asking for forgiveness from the people for wrongs that were committed.

Recently, on my visit to Sarawak to minister in our church camp, a couple from Australia who joined me had a similar experience. Caroline Rowlands shared that the Lord seems to lead her to a number of countries and places that were once colonized by the British. Since she and her family are from England, she repented before the people of Sarawak on behalf of the English for colonizing Sarawak through the White Raja (Raja Brooke) and killing a number of native patriots. Like the ministry done by Cindy Jacobs, Caroline stood in front of the people, relating what wrong had been done by their people in the past, and asking for forgiveness from the people who had been hurt. People came forward and shared the stories they had heard from their ancestors. They told about the evils and wrongs that came from the colonists. In order to repent, they spoke out, "On behalf of my ancestors and my people, I forgive you." Afterward they released blessings for America and England, and the wounds of the past were healed.

Since we have been doing similar identification repentance ministry over the years between various tribes in Sarawak such as the Iban, Bidayuh, Selako, Orang Ulu, and Chinese, we have witnessed tangible unity among believers of these people groups. Their villages have experienced development including good roads, electricity, and improvements to their water supply. Also, their children are doing well in studies. Currently more than twenty graduates have been produced from these communities besides those in tertiary institutions, whereas in the past there was almost none. Blessings are flowing into the communities, families, and children. Some of their children have risen up to be leaders in local government and state government agencies.

I will never forget Paul Ariga,[4] an intercessor from Japan. Paul humbled himself and asked those of us who had come from nations that Japan had invaded in the past and during World War II, and committed heinous atrocities to their people, to come forward and stand in the gap on behalf of our ancestors, so that he could ask forgiveness on behalf of his nation. Tears of repentance flowed while he asked for forgiveness. I remember the South Koreans were deeply moved, as they had been invaded and treated badly by the Japanese. Some of us represented Malaysia, and as we prayed and released forgiveness to our brother Paul, who was standing on behalf of Japan, we recalled the atrocities committed by the Japanese during the World War as told to us by our parents. As we prayed, we released God's blessings over the people and nation of Japan, and we commanded that the curse over the nation be broken.

Years later, when we met Paul Ariga again in Seoul, South Korea, for another conference, he was delighted and excited. He shared the blessings of his identification repentance. Paul said as an evangelist he always wondered why people in Japan did not respond by attending in the thousands to city-wide evangelistic rallies. He believed it was because of Japan's past evil and bloody deeds that God's blessings could not flow to the people so that they could respond to the gospel. However, after several years of humbling himself and repenting on behalf of his nation's past evil deeds, he began to see breakthrough. For the first time, his citywide evangelistic rallies drew tens of thousands of Japanese, and by the hundreds they responded to the gospel message.

We can break these controlling mind-sets and generational curses through acts of identification repentance that bring reconciliation and forgiveness so that people can be free to be powerful, successful individuals. This can be done by descendants who are Christians and intercessors standing in the gap on behalf of their ancestors. They can appeal to the blood of Jesus to cleanse the sins committed by their forefathers. Only then can they command the generational curses to be broken.

Daniel prayed and confessed his sins to God for his people. He identified himself with the sins of his ancestors, saying, "We have sinned and committed iniquity, we have done wickedly and rebelled, even by departing from Your precepts and Your judgments" (Dan. 9:5). Nehemiah prayed and confessed to God, "Both my father's house and I have sinned" (Neh. 1:6). As a result, God heard their prayers. He blessed their endeavors by releasing a series of events to restore their nation; bringing those people who were in exile back to their nation; and restoring their temple, the walls of Jerusalem, and the city. Thus their city and nation were restored and transformed from a wasted and broken place to that which God has purposed.

Weapons of binding and loosing and making decrees

Strongholds also need to be removed through warfare. Today, God is raising up apostles to work alongside prophets and intercessors. In the past, intercessors worked alone because leaders of the church who are apostles are not usually linked to these intercessors. As a result, these intercessory movements are not led by fathers or the spiritual leaders of a nation. Thus, the intercessors functioned separately, like outsiders, and did not feel appreciated because the fathers were not playing their role.

Then, along came prophets who began to prophesy things that upset the leadership, and as a result, they were rejected too. However, nowadays, God seems to be bringing intercessors to link up with prophets and apostles to work as a team. When a stirring or burden comes upon the intercessors, the prophets begin to verbalize and prophesy the word of God. Then the apostles exercise their authority by making decrees and providing the infrastructure and resources for the word of God to be realized. That is how nations can be touched and impacted by the power of God—through teamwork and oneness of heart.

> I will give you the keys of the kingdom of heaven, and whatever you bind on earth will be bound in heaven, and whatever you loose on earth will be loosed in heaven.
> —MATTHEW 16:19

In this instance, the "keys" of the kingdom of heaven are "binding" and "loosing." The same word "bind" is *deo* in Greek and was used by Jesus in Matthew 12:29. We must first bind the strongman before we can enter the strongman's house and plunder his goods—the souls of people.

In our case, we desired to plant churches among the Selako people of Sarawak, after identifying a number of strongholds among the people and in their communities. While in prayer, we "bound" the strongholds—spirit of death, spirits operating in the spirit mediums, or *bomohs*. For the Bidayuh people from *Podam* (village), we bound the spirit behind the huge black stone that the people worshipped. After that, we "loosed" God's spirit of salvation, healing, and miracles over the communities, villages, and the people. When we had healing and evangelistic meetings, we saw miracles and healings, and churches were started. Today, we have vibrant churches growing among several communities of Selako people, and there is no more spirit medium among the people. In Podam, the huge black stone was removed and taken away from the village, and a thriving church remains.

Spiritual mapping

Spiritual mapping is necessary in order for us to discern strongholds over nations as we are praying for social transformation. In this case, spiritual mapping is first provided by asking believers of those communities to do field research about the strongholds in their area; secondly, by discernment from the intercessors (that is, God will reveal to those of us who are praying the various strongholds, spirits, and powers that are controlling the people and their communities).

As we wrestle not against flesh and blood but against principalities, powers, rulers, and hosts of wicked spirits (Eph. 6:12), we must realize that behind every evil regime and unjust government are high ranking demonic spirits using humans as proxies to achieve their evil mandate—the degradation and destruction of good government. Most of these spirits may not have biblical names, but functional names can be easily identified. The spirit of corruption pervades in many nations stretching from South America, Africa, Asia, and into the former Soviet states. The spirit of injustice operates when good governance is ignored and democratic rights of the people are trampled. The spirit of mammon operates strongly in nations with thriving banking and business hubs. Unfortunately, rather than producing movies with good values, Hollywood and its entertainment industry are promoting immorality and appalling values globally; therefore, the spirit of immorality is now associated with Hollywood. Recently, some concerned Christians in the entertainment industry in Hollywood have had the burden to conquer the Arts and Entertainment sphere of influence for God. I'm sure we will be hearing more of such engagements in the near future.

3. RELEASE CORPORATE ANOINTING THROUGH CORPORATE UNITY AND PRAYER OF AGREEMENT

We all desire to do great things for God. However, so much more can be accomplished when we come together corporately with a unity not just in the sense of an organization, but with a bonding of hearts and relationships. Powerful breakthroughs happen in the spiritual realm when God's people come together as one.

God delights in corporate unity. Through it He releases His anointing and authority to make decrees, breaking the strongholds and powers of the enemy. This anointing that flows from corporate unity is both powerful and far reaching.

> That they all may be one, as You, Father, are in Me, and I in You; that they also may be one in Us, that the world may believe that You sent Me...that the love with which You loved Me may be in them, and I in them.
>
> —JOHN 17:21, 26

> Behold, how good and how pleasant it is for brothers to dwell together in unity! It is like the precious oil [anointing of the Holy Spirit] upon the head...It is like the dew [life-giving power of the Holy Spirit]...for there the LORD commanded the blessing.
>
> —PSALM 133:1–3

This must come to pass, not just in our church, but over the city and over the nations in this age and time.

In the past, intercessors did all the praying and interceding for the nation; but after so many years of various prayer movements, we are not seeing many results. The nation of Argentina, which has had at least fifteen years of prayer movement, went into an economic crisis, with inflation rising up into thousands of percent.[5] The same goes for Malaysia in the past—up until 2007, when a political tsunami took place. There was a major shift in the nation political landscape, with the opposition coalition winning five of the fourteen states and causing the ruling party to lose their two-thirds majority for the first time in history. What was the difference? This time the leading pastors or senior pastors of significant churches came together to pray for the nation joined by intercessors. That releases authority and power.

Leaders of churches need to realize this powerful principle and break down church walls. Let us not allow past differences, theologies, or practices to divide us anymore. We can set that aside and come together with oneness of heart to cry out to God for our cities and nations. Only then will we see a great leap forward in the church's impact and effectiveness.

Prayer of agreement

> Again I say to you that if two of you agree on earth concerning any-
> thing that they ask, it will be done for them by My Father in heaven.
> For where two or three are gathered together in My name, I am
> there in the midst of them.
> —MATTHEW 18:19–20

When two or three intercessors agree, it releases tremendous power in prayer; what more if two or three senior pastors were to agree together in their spirits and pray? However, when a whole regional or national pastors' network agrees together and prays, the result is exponentially greater.

Through the invitation of the Penang Pastors Network under the lead-ership of Dr. Andrew Chong, several pastors from the Central Region—including my wife and I, and several pastors from Sabah, an East Malaysian State—went to Penang Hill for a prayer retreat. Our common burden was to pray for our nation of Malaysia. This took place in late 2006, the year before the general election.

A number of pastors from the northern states were discouraged and were not optimistic with regards to our nation's direction and the political scenario. But as we came together to fellowship, share what the Lord was saying, and pray, the atmosphere changed, and faith came into the gathering of pastors. When each participant began to open up his or her heart and share, hearts were knitted together with the bond of the Holy Spirit. When we worshipped and prayed in the powerful presence of God and authority was released, we prayed the prayer of agreement and proclaimed decrees over our nation.

Several results transpired, including an Indian pastor whose church could not grow seeing a breakthrough with tangible increase in numbers. Several northern pastors were revived and began to meet together weekly rather than monthly. This became a prelude to greater participation and prayer for like-minded pastors throughout the nation to pray for our nation for the coming general election. That election was a watershed moment for our nation, because for the first time the ruling coalition party lost their majority in Parliament and could not change any law with regards to the Constitution as they pleased. Secondly, the opposition coalition won five states out of fourteen states for the first time.

On a personal level, I was invited to preach at Dr. Andrew Chong's. Since our hearts were knitted together in a deep way by the Holy Spirit, I felt an anointing when I ministered. Then a sign took place—manna-like, thin, irregular pieces of wafers began to fall at the front portion of the church where I was. The pastor shared how a woman sitting on the second row who was hungry for God experienced manna falling all over her hair. Supernatural manifestations of God occur when there is a true networking of hearts and lives through the Holy Spirit.

There is only so much one can do alone, but with heart-to-heart connections and teamwork, we can see phenomenal results. Peter could not cope with the enormous haul of fish God gave him, and he had to summon his friends to bring their boats alongside and help him. Peter would have lost his great harvest of fish if not for the others who came to his aid.

If we want to see a great harvest taking place and the nations being transformed, we have to go beyond our normal circles and practices. We need to be able to network with other spiritual fathers and ministries and work together to see the nations transformed. Let us be open to networking within our communities, cities, and nation, and even with ministries worldwide—not for the sake of building our own reputation or credibility, but to enable ourselves to expand the kingdom of God more effectively so that many more lives can be touched and transformed.

4. Develop Governmental Authority to Release the Decree of God as a Weapon of Spiritual Warfare

The church today is severely lacking in governmental authority to release the decrees of God. God raises up spiritual fathers and the apostolic ministry in order to align His church and define the roles and ministries within to take on their designated functions. The satanic realm already has its kingdom structure: principalities, powers, rulers, and spiritual hosts of wickedness.

However, in the kingdom of God, the structure is not in place! Our responsibility is to bring the kingdom of God structure to the earth.

Satan's hierarchy can be found in Ephesians 6:12, with "principalities," "powers," "rulers of darkness," and "hosts of darkness" or "hosts of evil spirits" under the headship of Satan.

God's government on earth is represented by apostles, prophets, evangelists, pastors, and teachers under the headship of Jesus Christ.

> So Christ himself gave the apostles, the prophets, the evangelists, the pastors and teachers, to equip his people for works of service, so that the body of Christ may be built up until we all reach unity in the faith and in the knowledge of the Son of God and become mature, attaining to the whole measure of the fullness of Christ.
> —EPHESIANS 4:11–13, NIV

Part of the problem is that for a long time, people did not recognize apostles and prophets as church governmental leaders that God has raised up into leadership. The Lord puts apostles and prophets in governmental positions in the spiritual realm. If God's governmental authority has not been properly established over the cities and nations, there will not be authority to pull down the powers of darkness. However, if God's government is in place and the authority of God rises to decree in the heavens, the demonic powers have no choice but to bow down, and the demonic strongholds will be pulled down.

Decrees over a nation

Once the spiritual government structure is in place, it paves the way for decrees to impact the nation. One very good example of this took place in the Philippines.

On March 3, 2007, in Manila, I proclaimed decrees over the nation of the Philippines. This was in the presence of many church leaders from various denominations, the leadership of the Christian Fellowship of the Central Bank of the Philippines, and about one thousand participants of the conference Touching Heaven, Changing Earth held at Philippines International Conference Centre.

Just before the nation of the Philippines had its national elections, I did the same again on May 13, 2007, at the Fathers of the Nation Gathering in

Malaysia in the presence of some five hundred intercessors, including senior pastors of numerous churches and the director of intercessors of the Philippines Movement Bishop Dan Balais, and his wife.

Various leaders were asked to pray for various issues including prayer for Malaysia and the government of Malaysia. David Demian and Gideon Chiu from Canada were also at the conference. I was requested to pray first for Indonesia and then for the nation of the Philippines. This was a day before the election in the nation of the Philippines for twelve out of the total of twenty-four Senate seats (midway between the presidential election, similar to the United States) and for a number of seats for Congress, mayors, and governors. The following are some of the decrees we made for that nation, and some of the outcomes:

The Decree: For godly men and women of integrity to be elected into office in greater numbers than ever before.

The Outcome: Of the twelve seats up for elections, ten of them fell into the hands of good people—eight of whom were specially selected by the churches. The other two were independent-minded senators of the administration. So one could say that it was a 12–0 win for good. For the first time in the nation's history, film stars failed to shine. A world boxing champ, though famous, lost his candidacy. An ex-election commission president lost. In one town, both candidates were known crooks and made money through illicit ways. At the last moment, a priest decided to run against all odds (and without the great financial resources that the other two had) and won. Eddie Villanueva's sons won; one as mayor and the other as congressman. Diwa Guinigundo's nephew won a Congress seat by a landslide.

In 2007, the Philippines elected a godly, just chief judge of the Supreme Court for the first time. He is a lay preacher who overturned two unjust rulings and shocked the nation, a clear demonstration of his righteousness and integrity.

The Decree: That those elected, regardless of their political affiliation, would stand on God's side to serve their nation, region, or community well; that they would not be corrupted for personal gain and status; and that the election would be carried out peacefully without resulting in any violence and anarchy or public disorder.

The Outcome: For the first time in many years, there was no rioting, killing, or burning during election time.

The Decree: Cheating and dishonesty will be stopped.

The Outcome: Those who intended to cheat in the elections were uncovered and exposed, and the TV stations' staff were following them everywhere. The paparazzi helped by keeping the news alive with the scandals.

The Decree: That the economy and peso will continue to rise and not depreciate.

The Outcome: In May 2005, the Philippine peso was 56 to 1 USD. As of December 2007, it went up to 46 to 1 USD.[6] When the oil prices increased, because of their currency strengthening, the Philippines did not have to raise the prices that much, and riots were averted. As of 2012, the peso had been one of the best performing currencies in the world and had gone up to below 44 to 1 USD.

The Decree: That the poverty level of the people will drastically fall.

The Outcome: The International Monetary Fund reported that the Philippines' poverty level dropped from 45 percent in 1994[7] to 27.9 percent in 2012.[8]

The Decree: That the nation of the Philippines will rise in stature and prosperity and enter into its God-given destiny: a truly blessed Christian nation that honors Judeo-Christian values.

The Outcome: The nation is taking its first steps toward owning that decree and rededicating itself to God. The new currency notes the phrase, "Blessed is the nation whose God is the Lord." In July 2011, the beautiful new currency notes of the Philippines were released, and I was given a commemorative set by the Deputy Governor Diwa Guinigundo. This is a start of many great things ahead.

CHAPTER 6
LINKING GENERATIONS

*T*HE JUNE 2008 Father's Day Sunday worship celebration was special. My wife, Lily, had invited Pastor Daniel Chan, and Pastor Nicholas Sim and his wife, Pastor Teresa, to pray for Lily and release her into the ministry.

By now Lily was past fifty-nine years of age and had been ministering with me for more than thirty-six years. Daniel Chan was her first pastor when she was a schoolgirl at Revival Centre Church in Singapore, where she gave her life to the Lord. Pastors Nicholas and Teresa Sim were her pastors when Pastor Daniel left for the United States to study at Fuller Theological Seminary. However, because she was such a quiet girl, the pastors took no notice of her, even though she had graduated from Singapore Bible College.

After we were married, Lily went for further study in Australia. When she returned, we decided that God was leading us to plant churches in Malaysia. Though God was using her in remarkable ways, Lily always expressed to me her longing to be connected with her previous pastors who had blessed her and ministered to her. One of her deepest desires was to be released by her pastors into the ministry to which God had called her.

When we first visited the United States of America in 1982, we visited Daniel Chan. Over the coming years, Lily was instrumental in encouraging and inspiring her pastor to return into the ministry. In early 2000, Daniel believed he had an assignment from God to go to Singapore and bring all those pastors and ministries from Revival Centre Church into a network called Unity Pastors. Lily went for the first meeting, and subsequently I was included. As a result, a great bonding was taking place between Pastors Nicholas and Teresa Sim and our ministries.

It was during one of the Unity Pastors meetings that Lily requested for Daniel, Nicholas, and Teresa to be present during the Father's Day meeting in 2008. During the worship service after Daniel Chan had preached, Lily shared with our church the significance of her request for prayer and to be released into the ministry by her previous generation of pastors. She believed that by the linking of three generations—like Abraham, Isaac, and Jacob—a synergy and generational blessings would be released. Since then, Lily has experienced and demonstrated a new boldness, freedom, and blessings in her ministry, which has stretched throughout Malaysia and into Singapore, the Philippines, and Australia, especially in Gold Coast and Melbourne.

This revelation did not come to us earlier, even though we had nearly forty years in our ministries. However, when Barbara Wentroble and Jim Hodges came into our lives as a spiritual covering for us and our ministries, we learned about this important revelation. As a result, Elijah, our biological and spiritual son, became closely linked with us and developed tremendous understanding concerning marketplace apostles, the eradication of poverty through business models, and marketplace ministries. His close links with Chuck Pierce, Dutch Sheets, and Cindy and Mike Jacobs reinforced such linking of generations to achieve kingdom purposes.

The Heart of a True Father

The spirit of Elijah is an outstanding role model, as he had a heart of a true father. He successfully trained up Elisha as his spiritual son and positioned him to be more successful than himself. Elisha received a double portion of Elijah's spirit, and Elisha finished what Elijah set out to do—destroying Ahab, Jezebel, and their descendants.

For those of us who have been spiritual fathers for years, it is about time we follow the same challenge that Elijah had in raising a new generation. I challenge leaders to groom the next generation of leaders and impart all that we know, to enable them to become more successful than ourselves. This younger generation carries the double portion of the Spirit and probably a greater vision than we carry. They are capable of transforming the nations during their lifetime. Our responsibility is to stand by and enable them to achieve the fulfillment of such a vision. As leaders, our satisfaction is to be a part of their successes rather than only using our sons to fulfill our vision. In this way, we are able to link the father and the son generations.

When spiritual fathers only use their sons to accomplish their own visions, it will result in separation. When sons feel there is not enough room to expand or work out their vision, they will leave their fathers and cause a break in the link between the relationships. Many breakups and separations in churches are caused by this reason alone. However, it is time for the hearts of the fathers to turn back to the children. Let the older leaders have a heart of a true father to impart all that they have. Let us make our sons more successful than ourselves. Help them to achieve their visions and their dreams.

One good example happened with Gideon Chiu in Canada when his three spiritual fathers stood by him to help bring his vision to pass. One of them was John White, who opened the door for him to minister in Quebec. Several years ago when a church crisis developed in Hong Kong, the leaders of the Chinese churches had placed much of the blame on Gideon Chiu, but John White came to Gideon's aid and was able to explain things and to cover him from the blame.

In a similar fashion, David Demian came along with a burden for nation transformation in Canada. Gideon Chiu, together with Albert Zehr, stood by David. Bob Birch, the apostle of prayer of Canada, had mentored David as a young man. To him, it was a joy to see David begin to rise up to his destiny. That is the heart of a true father.

I have personal relationships with Gideon Chiu and Albert Zehr, and I know their hearts; each of them definitely has the heart of Elijah to be a true father. I have known and watched David over a period of time, and I have seen how he relates with his fathers. I believe it leaves us with a very good model to follow.

RECONCILING FATHERS AND SONS

It has been said that a good father makes a good son, but the reverse is also true: a good son makes a good father.

A number of times, I have had to stand in the gap as a father to the sons where there has been hurt in these young lives. The deepest hurt for the sons is when their spiritual fathers used them to fulfill their own visions but did not nurture these sons or help them to come into their own vision and destiny.

Personally, I know this to be true. In the past, I was guilty of that same mistake. However, God began to open my eyes to see that my role as a father is to raise up sons that will be more successful than I am, and to help them to fulfill the destiny that God has for them.

Those of us in the older generation, fifty years of age and beyond, may still have a desire to see our nations come into transformation even if it may seem impossible to achieve for our generation. *But can we relook at our strategy and change our approach?* Why not link up with the next generation and watch the younger ones pursue visions greater than our own? Stand by them and plant seeds in their hearts to see nations become transformed. Nurture those seeds and help them grow. Let them avoid making the same mistakes we made. As our sons achieve success, we are also successful. What father would not be brimming with joy to see his sons receiving their scrolls during the graduation ceremony? These fathers may be farmers or those with little education, but it would still be their pleasure and joy to have raised up successful individuals in their lifetime. Remember that King David started out as a lowly shepherd boy. His father placed him in that position where he learned to become successful.

After over thirty years of ministry, one of the most vital lessons that I have learned is that we are not supposed to expect our sons to fulfill our own visions. Instead, we should be standing alongside them to fulfill their visions. At times, the visions of our sons can be bigger than our own, and even totally different things. If we do not understand this and begin to restrict them, there will be many relationship breakups and misunderstandings. We may feel hurt and betrayed, and perhaps even take the rejection of our vision personally; but on the other hand, it is that the sons have grown and feel the overwhelming need to fulfill their own God-given visions. They need to spread their wings and go after all that God has for them. A true father chooses to raise up sons who are more successful than themselves, even if they eventually do not want to carry on the family business or ministry.

A father-son relationship can be mutually enriching if both parties can value and respect each other. If the sons value tapping in to the wisdom and experience from the fathers to avoid mistakes made, they can save a great deal of unnecessary pain and setbacks. Armed with an inherited wealth of knowledge and experience from their fathers, they will be able to achieve more things within a shorter time frame. On the other hand, fathers also need to support the visions of their sons in any way possible, whether in spiritual, physical, or material aspects.

If the parents went through mistakes and failures for thirty or forty years, the children can pick it up vicariously within a few years and undergird their own lives with lessons learned from the parents' experiences. This is an advantage many fail to recognize. Continuing to build on knowledge gained by their fathers coupled with their own new experiences helps to prevent a repeat of the same mistakes, and so much more can be accomplished!

ABRAHAM, ISAAC, JACOB, AND JOSEPH: GENERATIONAL INHERITANCE

God is a transgenerational God. He is the God of Abraham, Isaac, and Jacob. Each successive generation was greater than the previous.

Abraham was already prosperous with a wealth of assets. When it came to Isaac's time, he inherited so much from his father that within one year he had the capacity to sow and reap one hundredfold. Genesis 26 states that he began to prosper greatly. When Jacob came into the picture, he left home with no capital because he was fleeing from his brother Esau. Interestingly, he still came back very wealthy, with the power to influence.

> In this way the man grew exceedingly prosperous and came to own large flocks, and female and male servants, and camels and donkeys.
> —GENESIS 30:43, NIV

That is outstanding success, and much more powerful than Isaac's, because Jacob started from point zero. Jacob had his father's blessings and birthright and had the confidence to know he could succeed. When the intergenerational link is established, blessings and inheritance always flow, and God's purposes for one generation will continue to be inherited by the next and the subsequent generations. God is able to use each generation to fulfill His purposes, but if there is a disconnect—through disowning, estrangement, or totally going against the will of God—it will have to start from scratch all over again.

In the time of Abraham, God said that He would bless him and make him a great nation:

> I will make you into a great nation, and I will bless you; I will make your name great, and you will be a blessing. I will bless those who bless you, and whoever curses you I will curse; and all peoples on earth will be blessed through you.
> —GENESIS 12:2–3, NIV

In Isaac's time, he sowed, and within that year he reaped one hundredfold.

> Isaac planted crops in that land and the same year reaped a hundred-
> fold, because the LORD blessed him. The man became rich, and his
> wealth continued to grow until he became very wealthy. He had so
> many flocks and herds and servants that the Philistines envied him.
>
> —GENESIS 26:12–14, NIV

When it came to the time of Joseph, not only did God bless everything
that Joseph put his hand upon with success, but he was also appointed as the
prime minister of the Egyptians, second only to Pharaoh in the land. The
transference of wealth during the first three generations eventually led to a
top position in government for the fourth generation. So, the two elements
are linked together; transference of wealth and governmental influence. (See
Genesis 39:23; 41:40–43.)

Joseph was able to cause transference of wealth to take place while in the
hands of Pharaoh. He actually bought all the lands in Egypt for Pharaoh.
God raised Joseph up to be in government for the purpose of nation transformation. He would be able to save his own family and land. The surrounding
nations had to come to Joseph for food, and he appears to have saved the
entire world from famine. These four generations going from strength to
strength led to a high position in government.

After Joseph, his sons became kings. Joseph and the next generation, his
sons, worked together; from that generation onward, both father and son
generations began to work together, and transference of wealth continued to
take place. At the same time, God continued to raise up kings and leaders of
nations from His children. From the twelve children came the tribes of Israel,
a nation among the community of nations in the world even to this day.

A present day example is George Otis Jr. His father, George Otis Sr.,
was general manager of Learjet before he came to know the Lord. He also
mentored his son very well. After knowing and working with George Otis
Jr. in the Spiritual Warfare Network for over fifteen years, I have found him
to be brilliant in his understanding of spiritual mapping and the transformation of cities. He is a strategic thinker for God's kingdom. He was so well
mentored by his father that instead of establishing himself in the corporate
world with his God-given talents and strategic mind and becoming rich, he
decided to channel all his energy and talent for God's kingdom purposes like
his dad. I pray many more fathers will mentor sons just like George Otis Sr.

CBN News—with the assistance of Dan Wooding, founder of ASSIST Ministries, a journalist and a close friend of George Otis Sr.—wrote of George's passing:

> George Otis, Sr., the man who pioneered Christian radio and television in the Middle East and influenced Christians around the world, died last weekend at the age of 90.
>
> George Otis, Sr., had been the general manager of LearJet before he received Christ as his Savior. Otis later founded the "Voice of Hope Radio Network" which can still be heard on every continent around the world. His energetic enthusiasm for the gospel helped him touch the lives of actors, athletes, and politicians, including Ronald Reagan...
>
> According to Wooding, another person who was deeply affected by George Otis, Sr., was entertainer Pat Boone, who said he and his wife were led into the experience of the Baptism of the Holy Spirit by Otis.
>
> [Boone told me in an interview] "I consider Harald Bredesen and George Otis to be my two Holy Spirit fathers. George was the one who led Shirley [his wife] and me into the Baptism of the Holy Spirit. Then he introduced me to Harald, his dear friend, and Harald just came right alongside like the Paraclete [the word comes from the Koine Greek word meaning 'one who consoles—a comforter' or 'one who intercedes on our behalf—an advocate' and led me into fuller commitment and understanding of God."...
>
> Steven Lawson, writing in *Charisma*, talked about the influence that both Bredesen and Otis had on Ronald Reagan. He said, "Bredesen was with [Pat] Boone and evangelist George Otis Sr. on another much-celebrated visit, this time with then-California Gov. Ronald Reagan. Otis told Reagan that if he remained faithful, he would someday occupy 1600 Pennsylvania Ave. With Otis on one side of Reagan and Bredesen on the other, the group joined hands and prayed."[1]

ELIJAH, ELISHA, AND THE YOUNG PROPHET: THE FINISHING ANOINTING

The linking up of generations enables the finishing anointing to take place. When a generation inherits the foundation and values established by the generation who came before them, the finishing anointing comes forth.

After Elijah had slain the prophets of Baal, Jezebel wanted to kill Elijah. At that time Elijah believed he was the only prophet of God left in the world, and when he learned his very life was being threatened, he became very depressed. Elijah ran away and was in much despair. (See 1 Kings 19). An angel appeared to him and told him to eat and drink in preparation for a forty-day journey. Elijah came to the same mountain where Moses had been, Mount Horeb. While in the same cave where Moses had been, the word of the Lord came to Elijah.

God then showed Elijah that He is bigger than what was in his heart. God caused a great wind to come and tear the mountains, but God was not in it. Neither was He in the earthquake or the fire. But God was in the still, small voice.

> Go, return on your way to the Wilderness of Damascus; and when you arrive, anoint Hazael as king over Syria. Also you shall anoint Jehu the son of Nimshi as king over Israel. And Elisha the son of Shaphat of Abel Meholah you shall anoint as prophet in your place.
> —1 KINGS 19:15–16

In the depths of Elijah's discouragement, something happened to him. Verse 11 of 1 Kings 19 says that the Lord passed by. God released a seed of a more powerful ministry into his life and impregnated him with a ministry that he had no knowledge about. While Elijah was thinking that it was the end of his journey, God was preparing him for bigger things.

Some of you may have been toiling for years and seeing minimal results, but God could be doing the same Elijah work in your life, impregnating you with a ministry bigger than you even imagine. Don't be discouraged. Remember that in our moments of discouragement, emptiness, and solitude, we are in the same position that Moses and Elijah were once in. By going through such discouragement, you become a prime candidate for God to birth a greater ministry through you and lift you up to a new level of ministry.

Elijah was indeed a successful father. When God anointed the prophet Elijah to be an apostle and father, he then raised up Elisha, who received a double portion of the anointing. The challenge is for spiritual fathers to raise spiritual sons more powerful than themselves, sons who can turn the nations around. Speak to our children and grandchildren. We may not have the privilege to rise up in all these areas, but they can. The future is before them. Never underestimate them and what they can become.

Though Elijah did anoint Elisha as prophet in his place, he was not able to anoint Jehu to be king over Israel and even the king of Syria, the king of a foreign kingdom. However, through that intergenerational link, he succeeded. This took place when Elisha instructed one of the young men to anoint Jehu to be king. God can use His prophets to recognize and anoint future government leaders of other nations. He is able to raise up prophets who are accurate and instrumental to bring about change in the nation.

The linking of three generations of prophetic leaders releases the finishing anointing. Look at the spiritual inheritance evident in the lives of Elijah, Elisha, and the young man who anointed Jehu to be king of Israel (2 Kings 9). The unnamed young man was a prophet from Elisha's school of prophets, one of Elisha's spiritual sons. When Elisha anointed Jehu, Jehu was empowered to rise up and destroy Jezebel, Ahab's descendants, and Baal worshippers. What Elijah began in his lifetime, the up-and-coming generations completed.

Today, the challenge is for spiritual fathers to raise spiritual sons more powerful than themselves, who are able to transform the nations for the kingdom of God.

GENERATIONAL BLESSINGS

Many business empires, those led by believers and unbelievers alike, share a similar element: one generation raises up wealth, stature, and reputation for the family and passes it on to the next generation, who then inherits and builds upon the work of the previous generation, bringing the business or reputation to higher levels of success.

YTL Corporation is a well-established Christian business empire in

Malaysia. The group was founded by Francis Yeoh's father, Tan Sri Dato'
Seri (Dr.) Yeoh Tiong Lay, after whom the group is named. Today, YTL
Corp is one of Bursa Malaysia's largest and most successful conglomerates
and together with its five listed subsidiaries has a combined Market Capi-
talization of about RM30.8 billion (US $10.15 billion). The company was the
first Asian non-Japanese company listed on the Tokyo Stock Exchange, and
it has been listed there since 1996.[2]

According to Wikipedia, "Amongst the group's key businesses are utili-
ties, operating and maintenance (O&M) activities, high-speed rail, cement
manufacturing, construction contracting, property development, hotels and
resorts, technology incubation, real estate investment trust (REIT), and
carbon consulting. YTL serves more than 12 million customers in over three
continents."[3] Over 70 percent of its revenue is from outside of Malaysia.

Francis Yeoh, CBE (Commander of the Order of the British Empire), the
current managing director of YTL, in his speech on the April, 9, 2009, stated:

> When I look at how God has richly blessed YTL, I quickly credit
> to our Lord Jesus all the honour and glory, to flee without haste the
> temptations of thinking *I had a part, even only a "little" part in it.*
> It is the Holy Spirit who reminds me that I am a mere steward of
> God's wealth. I am not the Master! I must only master sin![4]

Francis Yeoh is currently mentoring the next generation of leaders for
YLT including his children, nephews and nieces. A good number of them
have graduated from top universities like Oxford and Cambridge, and he
requires them to pursue a second graduate degree.

> "Eighty-five percent of YTL's business interests are outside of
> Malaysia," shares Yeoh. "Through the years of experience gathered
> over three generations, it is not good to be hostage to economic
> geography. So YTL has invested in territories where the rule of law
> is a way of life and we thrive in very competitive economies such as
> Britain, Australia and Singapore. For me, the best way for self pres-
> ervation is by being in economies that are very competitive so that
> you are never lulled into complacency." ...
>
> When asked what lessons in life he shares with his five children, he
> says, "My children know that it is important to encompass all areas of

what God reminds us—to do justice, do the right things and humility. It is true that this generation tasted more wealth than my generation but my children are not molly coddled and they are brought up with the concept that they are stewards of God's wealth. They don't own it and when much is given…much is expected of them."[5]

The inheritance of the generations is not just confined to family businesses. It can be the passing on of values, personality traits, experience, skills, and business acumen. If not for their fathers, these sons would not be where they are today. Instead of building anew, they have built upon their fathers' legacies and went higher and further than they otherwise could.

This same principle holds for spiritual matters. For example, I am constantly inspired by Pastor Bob Birch and David Demian's walk together. David stood by Bob as a son and built upon Bob's platform through the ministry of Watchmen for the Nations. Today, David is director of Watchmen for the Nations, a ministry that touches the destinies of many nations.

Starting with the nation of Canada, David knew that God's destiny for Canada is connected with her redemptive gift; that Canada is to be used of God for the healing of the nations. The Canadian flag carries the emblem of a maple leaf, indicative of Revelation 22:2: "The leaves of the tree were for the healing of the nations."

David started by calling a gathering of 2,300 people for a conference in Whistler, British Columbia, in 1994. No names of speakers were announced, but those of spiritual fathers and mothers. According to David Demian, "Spiritual fathers and mothers have a very important role to play in the body of Christ by providing a spiritual covering to protect the Lord's purposes."[6] He elaborated further that "spiritual fathers, who have the benefit of experience from their journey with God, can often serve these obstacles [which he went through when he was a young man ministering in Egypt] well before they come. And they also have wisdom on how to abort the enemy's attacks before they can even happen. If younger leaders could learn to walk under the covering of trusted spiritual fathers and mothers, we could avoid a lot of 'needless casualties of war' in our pursuits for God."[7]

A great emphasis is made on "corporate waiting on God and corporate hearing from God." Despite the fact that they didn't plan anything, the overwhelming presence of God and the freedom given to the Holy Spirit to orchestrate the meetings stirred the participants to intercession, repentance, declaration, and specific prophetic acts that they considered as spiritual "strikes in the ground" (2 Kings 13:18), thereby shifting the spiritual atmosphere of Canada. During this meeting, the First Nations people were moved to take rightful stewardship over the land and repent of idolatry. The second gathering was held in July of the following year in Victoria. In this meeting there was a time of repentance to reconcile the fathers to the children.

BABY BOOMERS, AND THE X, Y, AND Z GENERATIONS

Different generational groups coexist in this time: Baby Boomers, and the X, Y, and Z Generations. Each generation has its own distinctive traits and general outlook on life. If these groups can be linked in some way, and each generation can draw and learn from the rest, we will see fantastic results!

The Baby Boomers are the rebellious "flower" generation. They have an anti-establishment outlook. During the post-World War II period, many fathers died in the war, leaving mothers to raise up their children alone. The fatherless generation of the 1940s and 1950s left a legacy of the X Generation.

Known as a generation who has been in debt, members of Generation X, born from 1964 to 1981, wanted the same comforts that their parents enjoyed in their time. However, the seasons had changed, and they themselves could not attain what the previous generation had experienced. Lack of financial discipline and falling into debt have produced much anger and frustration. Left to fend for themselves, they felt abandoned as orphans.

Generation Y, born between the mid-1970s to the early 2000s, is known as the *why* generation. This generation does not simply do what you tell them to; instead, they often ask, "Why?" This IT-savvy and wired generation thrives on the online and cyber culture. Their mind-sets are heavily shaped by mass media, music, and the global culture. Most people of this generation are more influenced by their peers than parents.

Generation Z, born between the mid-1990s and late 2000s, is known as the *wireless generation*, an extremely high-tech people who lead very privileged childhoods. Nurtured with good food and technological advancement, the "net generation" gets into computers at a young age. Their toys are mostly digital, and they communicate via the Internet. They learn to think outside the box because of the accessibility of all kinds of knowledge through media and the Internet. They are great multitaskers and extremely creative thinkers. I predict that many inventions, ideas, and medical cures will come from them. This is the generation that will trigger a new, distinctive knowledge revolution.

When there is a link between one generation and the next, the younger generation can tap into the experience and wisdom of the older generation in order to quicken the pace of their own learning process so as to see their visions and aspirations fulfilled. Godly values can be passed down or inherited. Imagine all these top brains of the Generation Z working—but sadly, without good values! Many master crooks are emerging who are capable of inventing all sorts of computer viruses or hacking to steal. It is imperative that good values and principles be instilled in them at an impressionable age. They can be raised to be great men and women of God if the right seeds are planted in their lives at an early age.

Obama and his political leaders were skillful and strategic in utilizing the Internet to promote his theme, "Change We Can Believe In."[8] This not only resonated with the younger generation of voters but also was highly successful in raising record-breaking funds to run his 2012 campaign, including $690 million raised digitally (up from $500 million raised digitally in 2008).[9]

Twitter, the medium of movement, was used widely and effectively during the opposition protests in Iran after the re-election of Mahmoud Ahmadinejad. In the "Twitterverse," claims were made that the election was widely rigged.[10]

Communication of the gospel through Internet technology has caused countries and regions to be reached where the doors have been closed to the preaching of the gospel, including the Middle East countries. In areas where the gospel is hindered by persecution, the Internet plays a crucial role.

Spiritual fathers must link with the younger generation that is making use of information technology and can think outside the box. As city dwellers with global mind-sets, they are a global culture that is able to impact nations in a far greater way than we imagined.

CHAPTER 7
TOUCHING HEAVEN, CHANGING EARTH

*W*E TOUCH HEAVEN through worship. As we release the ministries of apostolic calling, marketplace apostles will move into a different level of transference of wealth. When we enter into God's presence through worship, intercession, prayer and fasting, transference of wealth and power structures begin to shift in the spiritual realm to affect world systems in the natural.

> After these things I looked, and behold, a door standing open in heaven. And the first voice which I heard was like a trumpet speaking with me, saying, "Come up here, and I will show you things which must take place after this." Immediately I was in the Spirit.
>
> —REVELATION 4:1–2

Jim Hodges, founder and president of the Federation of Ministers and Churches International, has a powerful insight into the importance of worship:

> We must see things from the throne's perspective before we can accurately see anything else. We must resist the tendency to see events in history without seeing the view from the throne of God first. While secularists and humanists refuse to do this, the church must not fail to do it![1]

The church must draw near to God, and from His throne will come forth revelations and strategies to touch many nations. As we enter into God's presence in worship as priests, we receive the divine mandate and strength to come forth as warriors for battle.

The Bible shows some examples of how we, as God's people, can touch heaven to change the earth.

JOSEPH: TRANSFORMING THE ECONOMY OF A NATION

Joseph was a dreamer, slave, and prisoner who became prime minister of the Egyptians. He had the economic anointing to save a nation (including his family) and the surrounding nations from economic disaster caused by famine, using divine wisdom to stockpile excess food that would be sold later at premium prices.

He learned to touch heaven in the midst of his experiences as a slave and prisoner. In his time of desperation and darkness, he had only one choice: turn to God! He kept his heart pure in the midst of false accusations and unrighteous treatment, punishment, and imprisonment. He forgave his brothers, counting what they meant for evil as something God meant for good. From a young age Joseph developed the prophetic anointing, prophetic revelation, and the gift of interpreting dreams. Ministering to Pharaoh with a sincere, humble heart, Joseph was promoted to the highest government office, the prime minister of the empire of Egypt. Even prison was a good training ground, as Joseph related with high government officials who had offended Pharaoh.

As a result, God released an economic anointing, wisdom, and strategy that would save the nation from economic crisis and bring transference of wealth to Pharaoh and his family. We need people like that. Too many nations around the world, including the continents of Africa and South America, are in dire need of such anointing.

As we enter into God's presence through worship, intercession, prayer and fasting, transference of wealth and power structures begin to shift in the spiritual realm to affect world systems in the natural.

It is my joy and honor to have a spiritual son, Diwa Guinigundo, who is the Deputy Governor of the Central Bank in the Philippines (BSP). I believe that he has the Joseph anointing to save the nation from economic downturn and suffering. He does not just have the economic wisdom but also the Joseph anointing, the prophetic unction and wisdom from God.

Cesar Arceo, leader of the BSPCF, had this to say in his article printed in the 25th Anniversary Magazine for Diwa Guinigundo's church, Fullness of Christ International Ministries, August 27, 2011:

The Bangko Sentral ng Pilipinas Christian Fellowship (BSPCF), a non-sectarian and non-denominational group of Bible-believing Christians, under the spiritual leadership of Deputy Governor and Diwa C. Guinigundo soared to the next spiritual level by going beyond the walls of the Institution to the Body of Christ. This Holy Spirit inspired movement started on September 15, 2005, when Touching Heaven, Changing Earth was launched in PICC, the premier convention centre in Manila.

It envisions "seeing the nation worship Jesus" by
    expanding the Kingdom of God;
    kicking the devil out of the marketplace; and
    transforming our beloved nation.

Seminars and conferences are being conducted for free. The first conference was held at PICC Plenary Hall having guest speakers from the USA and Malaysia. Another one was held at the BSP Assembly Hall attended by more than 1,000 leaders and pastors.

Seminars were held in Davao, Cebu, Tagbilaran, Dumaguete, San Fernanado LU, Urdaneta, Legaspi, Naga and the latest was in Cabanatuan on 16 August 2011. Diwa shared the message by preaching the latest bulletin from Heaven for the Body and the latest economic condition and strategies for the country. We are blessed to be a blessing. To God be the Glory! Touching Heaven, Changing Earth is gathering momentum presently, and it is fast becoming a national movement for the transformation of the nation of the Philippines. By 2012, Touching Heaven, Changing Earth Movement provincial conferences has reached 14 cities including San Fernando, La Union; Davao City; Cebu City; Bohol, Negros Oriental; Pangasinanl Albay; Naga, Camarines Sur; Nueva Ecija, San Jose, Nueva Ecija; Batangas City; Olongapo City; and Puerto Princesa, Palawan. Since then, hundreds of churches represented by hundreds of pastors and elders and church leaders were reached through similar conferences.

In the brochure "Touching Heaven, Changing Earth Movement" published by Bangko Sentral ng Pilipinas (BSP) Christian Fellowship, Contact: Bro. Cezar Arceo, email czarceo@yahoo.com, these brothers and sisters from the Central Bank equivalent to U.S. Federal Reserve, took prophetic words delivered by God-sent prophets seriously including the word given by Cindy Jacobs: "The next two years will be critical. The spirit of corruption will be pulled down. There will be a release of spirit of truth and righteousness. The Philippines will be one of the wealthiest nations on Earth. The spirit of poverty will be broken. Out of darkness, there will be a transformation movement that will be a world model. The Filipino people need to fast and pray without ceasing. Love your nation!"

It is also stated in the brochure: "The task is for the church to truly take leadership in the governance of the Philippines. If the church is united, the people of God can elect righteous, just, competent, and honest leaders in both the national and local level, help appoint equally righteous, just, competent, and honest leaders in the judiciary and the executive departments of Government. The church should always be the gatekeeper of the Philippines; not sparing words of admonition to those who are abandoning God's principles, nor encouraging words to those who keep to the statutes of the Living God." Therefore, the thrust of this Movement: "to unite the body of Christ and help redeem the Philippines from the oppressive spirit of poverty and disunity. Touching the heart of God can change the fate and destiny of the Philippines."

It is also my privileged honor to have spent time with Eduardo Villanueva prior to the Philippines elections in 2004 to share with him my heart to see the nation transformed. After my talk with him, he felt so affirmed that he took it as confirmation that he should run for president. Though he did not win, he paved the way for many to follow in his footsteps.

Subsequently, others also began running for positions in government, such as congress and mayorship, with success. Eddie also tried running for president again in the 2010 elections. Although he did not win, this is an outstanding example of a standard bearer to the people of the nation. I did ask Brother Eddie Villanueva concerning some of the good things that happened to his nation and his own life as a result of him running for the presidential election though he did not win. He replied the following by e-mail:

> The experience gave a unique and unusual opportunity for Bible-believing Christians to perform an act of national intercession and "standing in the gap." Everywhere in the campaign, God's name was honored and the principles of His Word were sought to be applied to national governance, particularly in addressing the country's

problems and challenges. Prayers were made for the blessing of the nation in major places of the archipelago. What this achieved was that it was recorded in heaven, on earth, and in history, that many of God's children in the Philippines were willing to live by, live out, and live up to God's precepts in the realm of governance and politics in the country, and were united in blessing the land. I believe this had and has an intercessory effect on the country that only heaven can tell in eternity.

It also forced the nation to grapple with the reality of Bible-believing Christians in their midst. My mere participation in the electoral exercise was a decisive and emphatic statement that Christians are around, that they will act to campaign for righteous leadership in the hope of espousing a good and godly governance, and that they will dare whatever odds, if only to show their obedience to God.

Personally, it was the humbling opportunity to demonstrate my absolute Abrahamic obedience to God, together with all the faithful supporters of God's righteous call in our nation. That was the joy that sustained me throughout the exacting experience that I could call the crucible of my faith. In my heart of hearts, I knew no greater reward than the certainty that, before the eyes of God and history and eternity, I obeyed the Lord at all costs.

All told, what the electoral participation achieved was an assertion of presence, a registration of the willingness and boldness of believers to make a stand for their God in open society.

By any standard, it was well worth it all.

—Bro. Eddie Villanueva

The question is, how could it have been the will of God for Brother Eddie to run when he ended up losing the election? Since DVDs were distributed by thousands showing Cindy Jacobs declaring, "Brother Eddie, it is the will of God for you to be president," we need to offer a sincere explanation rather than ignore the issue. To some it looks like a false prophecy because it did not come to pass.

To be fair, Cindy Jacobs did emphasize on the same DVD that an army of David must arise from the body of Christ to take down Goliath (which means poverty and corruption). The body of Christ at that time was divided, and only some rose up. True, prophecies are conditional, meaning there are conditions to be fulfilled before the prophecies come to pass. However, I have another perspective from the Scriptures.

In 1 Samuel 8:4–5 the elders of Israel gathered together to ask Samuel for a king. Though Samuel was displeased, he prayed to the Lord, and the Lord said to Samuel, "Heed the voice of the people in all that they say to you; for they have not rejected you, but they have rejected Me, that I should reign over them" (v. 7).

It was definitely the will of God for a judge to be appointed so that God would still be King over Israel; however, it was the desire and will of the people to have a human king like other nations had. What the elders of Israel asked for was not the will of God, but God told Samuel to give in to their request. As far as God was concerned, they had rejected Him.

Having Saul as king was not the will of God but rather the choice of the people. Brother Eddie Villanueva was God's choice for president, but the body of Christ as a whole—except for certain sections—could not accept it. Compare this to the past, when Fidel Ramos ran for president. The church was united at that time, and Ramos became the first Protestant president— and a good one—for the Philippines. Eddie Villanueva was President Ramos's spiritual advisor at that time. Although he did not win the election, Eddie knows he obeyed God, and his conscience is clear.

It was God's will for Moses to enter into the Promised Land, but he forfeited it through disobedience. When the Israelites were in Kadesh Barnea, it was God's will for them to cross over to Israel—probably only an eleven-day journey—but rather than listening to the minority reports of Caleb and Joshua, the people were demoralized by the reports from the ten spies concerning the giants. Caleb said, "Let us go up at once and take possession, for we are well able to overcome it" (Num. 13:30). But the rest of the spies said, "We are not able to go up against the people, for they are stronger than we" (Num. 13:31).

Once when I went to the Philippines, I made a call to Diwa's nephew Magtanggol "Magi" Guinigundo and encouraged him to run for Congress with an attitude of humbleness and submission before God, and to declare his candidacy to the people around him, asking them to support him. This man had lost the bid for mayorship during the last round of elections, and running for Congress was a step higher. In 2007, Magi's dad told me that his son had won, and that I was the one who prophesied to him that if he ran he would win. And win he did—with a landslide of 70 percent of the votes!

Do we really want to see the nations transformed? Then first we must touch heaven! The apostolic and prophetic must be released into the churches of these nations. We must move in intercession and restore the spiritual things that God has for the church. The church must be fully equipped to function in worship, intercessory, prophetic, and apostolic dimensions so that God's people may learn to touch heaven and create impact on earth.

Insulated but not isolated

We must be insulated but not isolated from the world. The church is like a boat in the waters of the world. As long as the water does not flow in, the boat is still good for travel and able to move into God's destiny. However, Jesus taught in the parable of the leaven that we should not just be insulated from the world. We must think afresh about how to influence our culture and society with godly values and principles.

Nowadays, many protective parents keep their children so isolated from the world that they become social misfits. When they grow up, they often cannot cope with the pressures and realities of the world. A generation of people must be raised up who will dare to face the world like an army of God whose eyes are transfixed like a lion watching its enemies. They can be trained to face challenges and bring restoration to many aspects of the world systems for the Lord. Let us pray for the day when our future generations begin to restore the businesses, entertainment, and the mass media for the Lord.

God gave Joseph the strategy to stockpile and sell food at a premium price to transfer wealth to his government. All the people sold their land, and Pharaoh became the richest land owner of that period. With such economic wisdom God can cause transference of wealth to take place for His people.

Turning the nation around both in the natural and the spiritual

In Africa, many nations continue to suffer from famine and disaster. During my days as a Bible school student in Australia, I remember going from house to house collecting donations for Ethiopia and other African nations. Thirty years later, funds continue to be collected for the same causes. The African nations are under generational curses that need to be repented of, and many do not know it.

Food aid programs are not the answer, though they serve well in providing immediate needs. The United Nations is not the answer in the long term.

Giving money to them is not the answer either. A total, holistic approach—in both the spiritual and the natural, through marketplace apostles with the ability to bring transformation—is needed to help position God's people in government, education, and agriculture.

Intercessors should be sent to pray over marketplace apostles, and prophets sent to prophesy over the land and steer them toward repentance and spiritual strength. Christian businesspeople have an equally important role to show what can be done in the name of God: educate, provide employment, raise productivity in the nation, and turn the nation around both spiritually and economically. Perhaps equipping and teaching the locals to own the vision of nation transformation will be far more powerful than attempting to change it directly. Then nation transformation can take place in far greater measure.

The great Argentina revival in the 1990s reaped a mighty harvest of souls after much spiritual warfare. Unfortunately, the nation went into an economic downturn after that, and the currency was devaluated. Civil unrest and political corruption were happening in the country. My personal observation is that the nation's problems were caused because the church governmental structure and the fivefold leadership of that nation were not properly set in place to counter the demonic forces of the nation. The leaders of the Argentina revival were pastors and evangelists. Without a leadership composition that included apostles, they did not have full corporate unity and apostolic covering.

Contrast that with Guatemala, where the apostles took a leadership role in the Spiritual Warfare Movement. They organized conferences, inviting educators from the United States to come. They established top-class schools. They brought in experts from the business world. The apostles could mobilize resources in a big way. They came together as gatekeepers of the nation and were able to speak to the demonic realm to pull down its structures. The leaders of the nation stepped into their authority in the land. In the church, apostles were the leading structure with designated power and authority over the nation. When they spoke to tear down demonic structures, it brought results.

To have apostles leading the way is what we want for many nations in the future. God can anoint many Josephs in our midst. Among the Asian countries, Cambodia, Laos, and Myanmar are opening up and in need of the Lord. The continent of Africa has insurmountable conditions, with genocide, civil unrest, AIDS, and famine making many parts a living hell. Something substantial must be done to begin turning nations.

DANIEL: TRANSFORMING THE LAW
AND POLITICS OF A NATION

Daniel was the perfect example of one placed by God in a strategic position of government to transform the nation's laws. We need to raise up more Daniels among the next generation. Before this can happen, the young people and children must be taught to honor the Lord in all that they do, whether in their studies or professions, as we see in Daniel's example:

> The king assigned them a daily amount of food and wine from the king's table. They were to be trained for three years, and after that they were to enter the king's service.
> Among those who were chosen were some from Judah: Daniel, Hananiah, Mishael and Azariah. The chief official gave them new names: to Daniel, the name Belteshazzar; to Hananiah, Shadrach; to Mishael, Meshach; and to Azariah, Abednego.
> But Daniel resolved not to defile himself with the royal food and wine, and he asked the chief official for permission not to defile himself this way.
> —DANIEL 1:5–8, NIV

Young people need to learn how to touch God through their daily communion with Him, and make a resolution to stand for Him in the face of trials and persecutions for His name's sake. They must learn how to activate the prophetic gifts within them in order to hear from God and carry His vision.

A godly attitude and a posture of humility

Daniel had a spirit of servanthood, and the Babylonian king he served saw that. If we want to serve those in authority, we must have the same spirit of servanthood. Daniel lived under an oppressive government with an anti-God law, but he maintained a godly attitude and a posture of humility even when God's judgment came upon King Nebuchadnezzar. When asked to interpret a dream of judgment upon the king, Daniel hoped it was not the king for whom the judgment was meant. For us to minister to rulers in positions of great power and authority, we need to be like Daniel, who displayed an understanding of protocol and a heart of compassion.

God's people must have a full awareness of the reality of the enemy yet fully assert their authority within the kingdom of God. We must learn to engage in spiritual warfare against demonic powers and rulers. At the same time, we need to be willing to serve and speak to the leaders of our nation with a right attitude. The result will be what Daniel experienced in his time. The king changed the law of the land in favor of Daniel and his God.

> The people who know their God shall be strong, and carry out great exploits.
>
> —DANIEL 11:32

Even when asked to bow down to idols, Daniel did not harbor anger or bitterness toward the king. When King Nebuchadnezzar had a terrible nightmare of his own downfall, Daniel did not rejoice that God was finally dealing with the king. When Daniel spoke to King Nebuchadnezzar, he did not wish that the dream would be about the king but rather that the dream would be about his enemies. Yet in verse 22 he went on to explain that the tree was the king, and that just as the tree was chopped down, the same would happen to him.

> Then Daniel (also called Belteshazzar) was greatly perplexed for a time, and his thoughts terrified him. So the king said, "Belteshazzar, do not let the dream or its meaning alarm you."
>
> Belteshazzar answered, "My lord, if only the dream applied to your enemies and its meaning to your adversaries! The tree you saw, which grew large and strong, with its top touching the sky, visible to the whole earth, with beautiful leaves and abundant fruit, providing food for all, giving shelter to the wild animals, and having nesting places in its branches for the birds—Your Majesty, you are that tree! You have become great and strong; your greatness has grown until it reaches the sky, and your dominion extends to distant parts of the earth."
>
> —DANIEL 4:19–22, NIV

Daniel warned that Nebuchadnezzar would be driven to live like the beasts of the field, eating grass like oxen and wet with the dew of heaven for seven times, until the time would be completed. Then he advised the king that his kingdom would be assured. Unfortunately, King Nebuchadnezzar did not heed his advice, and the judgment of God came to pass according to his dream. (See Daniel 4.)

Incidentally, in our modern times, Iraq—the country presently representing Babylon—also had a similar case in the form of Saddam Hussein, their former president. In spite of his arrogance and defiance against many countries, he ended up hiding in a primitive cave and was sentenced to death by hanging through Iraq's judicial system. In contrast to Nebuchadnezzar, who eventually repented, Saddam Hussein did not repent.

At the end of the time, Nebuchadnezzar acknowledged that God's dominion is everlasting from generation to generation and that He does according to His will in the armies of heaven and the inhabitants of the earth (Dan. 4:34–35). The king praised God and acknowledged that God is able to strip anyone who walks in pride, from the lowest to the highest, of presumptuous confidence. Through Daniel's intercession and advice for the king, Nebuchadnezzar was given a chance to seek God and gain prophetic insight to the dream, and was able to walk through his experience with a revelation of God's power and goodness. As a result, the whole kingdom was transformed because the king was transformed.

> At the end of that time, I, Nebuchadnezzar, raised my eyes toward heaven, and my sanity was restored. Then I praised the Most High; I honored and glorified him who lives forever.
>
> His dominion is an eternal dominion; his kingdom endures from generation to generation. All the peoples of the earth are regarded as nothing. He does as he pleases with the powers of heaven and the peoples of the earth. No one can hold back his hand or say to him: "What have you done?"
>
> At the same time that my sanity was restored, my honor and splendor were returned to me for the glory of my kingdom. My advisers and nobles sought me out, and I was restored to my throne and became even greater than before. Now I, Nebuchadnezzar, praise and exalt and glorify the King of heaven, because everything he does is right and all his ways are just. And those who walk in pride he is able to humble.
>
> —DANIEL 4:34–37, NIV

When the three Hebrew boys Shadrach, Meshach, and Abednego refused to worship the golden image of the king through a wicked decree, they maintained a pure heart toward the king and did not protest against him. They were steadfast in their stand to worship God only. When the furious king cast them into a fiery furnace for their disobedience, they were unharmed. The astonished king saw not only three but four persons, and the fourth one had the appearance of the Son of God. When the king summoned the three of them, amazingly even the smell of fire was not on them. Then the king decreed that anyone who defamed the God of heaven would be punished. Nation transformation took place, and God's signs and wonders shifted the king's mind-set. The law was changed, and the three were given places of influence in the government.

> At this time some astrologers came forward and denounced the Jews. They said to King Nebuchadnezzar, "May the king live forever! Your Majesty has issued a decree that everyone who hears the sound of the horn, flute, zither, lyre, harp, pipe and all kinds of music must fall down and worship the image of gold, and that whoever does not fall down and worship will be thrown into a blazing furnace."
>
> —Daniel 3:8–11, niv

When these three young men made their stand for God, He moved on their behalf and changes happened. Those serving in government must have the same spirit as Daniel to be effective marketplace apostles or prophets for people of influence. Because they are called to government and places of influence, God grants them authority. The prophetic anointing and revelation will come upon them, including the gift of interpretation of dreams. It is interesting to note that these gifts were not just operating in the Sunday service or in the nuclear church but in the marketplace through the marketplace apostles. These people in the Bible were serving in an oppressive regime, even a dictatorial one, with draconian laws that were against their faith and beliefs, but God still transformed the king and the laws of the land and placed these people in high positions of government.

I once had the privilege to dine with the right-hand man of President Ramos of the Philippines. Suddenly he asked me if I had a word to give to the president. I had no premonition that I would be asked, but I was ready!

We must live in a higher level of moving in prophetic giftings. The question is, *Are we ready when the opportunity comes to give the word of God?*

The ability to make an impact goes beyond just personal prophecy to stir up and bless. Ultimately, we must be used by God to touch those in places of authority and speak change into their hearts to shift the nations. We must move prophetically in anticipation of the day when such powerful anointing shall enable us to minister to leaders of our land, in the government, the corporate world, and in various areas of influence.

Evangelism alone is never enough. We must move into other new areas to which God has called us. Thus we need to instill the seed and vision of how God can use each one of us to the bigger cause of seeing how the destiny of our nations can be fulfilled as an essential component of discipling new believers and children. By doing so, we are preparing God's people as instruments to fulfill God's purposes for the nations. Our curriculum to train and disciple should not stop at winning souls but should also include nation transformation.

ESTHER: SAVING A NATION

Queen Esther saved a nation from death and destruction because:

+ Firstly, she learned to touch heaven by seeking the face of God through fasting and praying.
+ Secondly, she risked her life at the right time and right place.

> If you remain completely silent at this time, relief and deliverance will arise for the Jews from another place, but you and your father's house will perish. Yet who knows whether you have come to the kingdom for such a time as this?
>
> —ESTHER 4:14

+ Thirdly, she was prepared to die.

> Go, gather all the Jews who are present in Shushan, and fast for me; neither eat nor drink for three days, night or day. My maids and I will fast likewise. And so I will go to the king, which is against the law; and if I perish, I perish!
>
> —ESTHER 4:16

Queen Esther had a good attitude toward the king—no tempers, strikes, or boycotts against the king when the oppressive decree to kill her people came forth. Instead, she sought the face of God and was willing to give up her life for the cause. Rather than complaining up front about the draconian law, she arranged for a banquet for the king and Haman. Haman, the schemer behind this ethnic cleansing of the children of Israel, thought he would be given a great reward, but Esther gradually began to expose his evil intentions before the king, all the time maintaining goodwill and favor with the king. As a result, the decree was changed, Haman was hanged, and the lives of her people were spared.

Esther displayed honor and respect for the king through her actions, words, and conduct. Likewise, if those of us in government are to engage with people of authority, a godly protocol and attitude must be maintained amidst adversities and unjust laws.

Whether you are a doctor, banker, teacher, businessman, or even in government or the judicial system, do not consider it merely as a profession. God positioned you for a specific time and purpose so that when the right occasion comes, you can respond like Esther. When the time and opportunity arises, we must be ready to play our part, where we are and in the place where we are positioned.

NEHEMIAH: REBUILDER OF A NATION

From just being a cupbearer to King Artaxerxes, who ruled over the Persian empire, Nehemiah was appointed as governor over Judah. It all started because of his burden to rebuild the city of Jerusalem, which lay in ruins.

As cupbearer to the king, he had the ruler's respect and trust. The king's life actually depended upon him. Assassination of kings by way of poisoning their food and drinks was common in those times, and every king had his enemies. Nehemiah was the king's fall guy, his food and wine taster—an important role. One of the protocols he had to observe was to be cheerful all the time, so much so that when the king realized his cupbearer was sad, he was concerned. Nehemiah was willing to open his heart to tell the king of the legitimate concern for Jerusalem, the land of his fathers. Even though it was a breach of protocol, Nehemiah was willing to open up his heart to share what was troubling him.

Nehemiah had definitely found favor with the king, and therefore the king was willing to release him for a period of time to fulfill the desires of his heart and see the walls of Jerusalem rebuilt. The king truly appreciated the way Nehemiah honored and respected the king; he even appointed Nehemiah as the governor over Judah! He reigned as governor for thirteen years. This was the fruit he reaped after sowing many years of faithful service and sacrifice for the king.

If we can serve and be of value to those in authority and for our nation, we will be noted. A high level of trust is gained from those we deal with. The time will come when our burden for God's work will be recognized and much favor shall be given to us to facilitate all that God wants to carry out in our nation. But first we must serve with both diligence and distinction in order to command that kind of respect and trust.

When Fidel Ramos became president of the Philippines in the 1990s, he asked Eddie Villanueva to serve as his spiritual advisor. The nation prospered greatly during the six years of Ramos's presidency (1992 to 1998). President Ramos played a major role in the People Power Revolution that caused the overthrow of the dictator Marcos. President Ramos brought the nation to a new height of prosperity, curbed corruption, and brought major development to the nation. He left behind a great legacy of being a good president.

GIDEON: WINNING THE WAR

Gideon believed that God could deliver and transform his nation, but he could not understand why He was not making it happen:

> The Angel of the Lord appeared to him, and said to him, "The LORD is with you, you mighty man of valor!"
>
> Gideon said to Him, "O my lord, if the LORD is with us, why then has all this happened to us? And where are all His miracles which our fathers told us about, saying, 'Did not the LORD bring us up from Egypt?' But now the LORD has forsaken us and delivered us into the hands of the Midianites."
>
> Then the LORD turned to him and said, "Go in this might of yours, and you shall save Israel from the hand of the Midianites. Have I not sent you?"

So he said to Him, "O my Lord, how can I save Israel? Indeed my clan is the weakest in Manasseh, and I am the least in my father's house."

And the LORD said to him, "Surely I will be with you, and you shall defeat the Midianites as one man."

—JUDGES 6:12–16

Sometimes, we also ask why we look like a "defeated nation" and why we have to be the ones running away from problems and enemies. Where are the miracles that our fathers spoke about? Gideon was very burdened with the fact that he was captive in the hands of the Midianites, but God called him a mighty man of valor because he refused to accept the seemingly hopeless condition he was in. He believed that God could reverse the situation and cause great miracles and deliverance to occur. He refused to accept the condition of the day, or the defeat.

I can almost hear God saying to Gideon, "Do you know why there are no miracles like your father talked about? Because there was nobody I could use. But now for the first time, I found you; someone I can use. You have something I can use, because you, a mighty man of valor, have refused to accept the status quo. You believe I can do great things, and refuse to accept defeat. You always believed that I could reverse it and do great things with signs and miracles. Because of that, you are a great man of God, a mighty man of valor."

Can we be like Gideon and allow ourselves to be used mightily, as insignificant as we think ourselves to be? Dare we believe for the same miracles that happened in the days of Moses to take place here and now? Do we believe that God has the final say in victory for our nation?

RIGHT PEOPLE, RIGHT TIMING

God can use you to fulfill His mighty purposes, even if you think you are a nobody. It is not what you have but what God has that counts. It is not how much power you have but how much power God holds. His will and purposes supersede even your weaknesses to make great things happen! God will take away all fear and discouragement from us and replace it with a victorious, conquering spirit that the devil cannot defeat. Let us live out that word, "The Lord is with you, you mighty man of valor."

Strength in numbers does not mean anything to God. In the Book of

Judges, Gideon only had three hundred, although he wished that he had three hundred thousand. But God still gave him victory over his enemies. Daniel and his friends were only a team of four, but that was the critical mass needed to tilt the balance of power and reverse laws. When God looks at your heart, can He see something mighty? God does not look at numbers, but He wants the heart. If we do not have a heart for God, He cannot move through us. He is waiting for the right people and timing to swing things into action.

Pastor Chew, the leader of Sidang Injil Borneo (SIB) KL in Kuala Lumpur, once told me that the SIB churches were pioneered by three Australian missionaries in 1928. Today, there are approximately five hundred SIB churches in Sabah and another five hundred in Sarawak. With over 500,000 members in these two states, SIB is now the largest Christian denomination in Malaysia next to the Roman Catholic Church. Why? Because three Australian missionaries dared to make a difference and were determined to change the nation.

Let us raise up men and women who are godly and not corrupted who will serve the nation with pure hearts when they come into positions of power. It begins by raising the next generation of young people right now. Implant the right values and teach them to dedicate themselves to the purposes of God the way Daniel did, to resolve in their hearts not to defile themselves along the way. Give them the best education, equip them with the best skills, pray for them, and stand with them until they become successful and are placed in positions of power. Then, they can effect change.

Can you imagine hundreds of God-fearing people serving in Congress, and dozens of them in the Senate or serving in local communities as mayors? They will be in places of influence to swing the direction of government policies and laws onto the right path. If people with the Joseph anointing carry out God's strategy and develop good economic models in business, small-to-medium industries, and agriculture, they will be able to contribute toward steering their nation's course of economic progress. Many policies, financial provisions, and jobs can be created to help eradicate poverty. We need to establish good education systems to provide excellent education.

Nation transformation is the key for God to turn the people back to Him. Now more than ever it is a major strategy in mobilizing His church to reach the world.

CHAPTER 8
The ACTION PLAN *for*
NATION TRANSFORMATION

*A*N OUTSTANDING MODEL of someone used by God in history for societal transformation is William Wilberforce. He started his political career as an Independent Member of Parliament in 1780 and became leader of the movement to abolish slave trade.

> In 1787, he came into contact with Thomas Clarkson and a group of anti-slave-trade activists, including Granville Sharp, Hannah More, and Charles Middleton. They persuaded Wilberforce to take on the cause of abolition, and he soon became one of the leading English abolitionists. He led the parliamentary campaign against the British slave trade for twenty years until the passage of the Slave Trade Act 1807...
>
> In later years, Wilberforce supported the campaign for the complete abolition of slavery, and continued his involvement after 1826, when he resigned from Parliament because of his failing health. That campaign led to the Slavery Abolition Act 1833, which abolished slavery in most of the British Empire; Wilberforce died just three days after hearing that the passage of the Act through Parliament was assured.[1]

Currently, in the United States, Dutch Sheets, Hope Taylor, and Cindy Jacobs are a few of those whom God has raised to transform the nation. These are precious servants of God whom I have known and had relationship with over the years. They have a definite assignment from God to see the United States of America transformed.

Hope Taylor, who heads the International Leadership Embassy (ILE) based in Washington DC, has a ministry partnership with Christian International, led by Bishop Bill Hamon; and the Federation of Ministries and Churches International (FMCI), led by Apostle Jim Hodges. I attended the

FMCI Conference when ILE was launched some years ago. Below is the statement of its vision and ministry.

The Vision

To establish an apostolic-prophetic center to envision and educate the Body of Christ with a Kingdom Governmental strategy to transform America and the nations. To "influence the influencers" in the church and Civil Government.

The Ministry

International Leadership Embassy will function with an apostolic authority to establish a Kingdom deposit and influence in the governmental arena that will transcend the territorial boundaries of the United States to affect many other nations. As with the Prophet Daniel, who was raised up with a spiritual governmental authority to influence the civil government, ILE will bring a kingdom influence into Washington DC in the following ways:

- Hosting and coordinating harp (worship), bowl (prayer) and crown (authority) worship and spiritual warfare teams.

- Hosting and coordinating prayer/intercession teams at strategic sites and events.

- Establishing the Institute on Government and Foreign Affairs to teach American and foreign government leaders, and Christian leaders biblical principles of government, public policy and worldview.

- Ministering to the foreign diplomatic staffs who serve their countries in 180 national embassies.

- Hosting and coordinating "sessions" where church leaders interface with civil government leaders for the purpose of societal, cultural and national transformation.

- Converging and building relationships with key national leaders and ministries who serve in D.C. to advance the Kingdom of God.

- Develop a special operations ministry to facilitate strategic assignments related to D.C. and the nation.

- Establish a ministry of integrity from which will be released a prophetic voice to the church and the nation.[2]

So, how do we actually go about causing nation transformation to take place? Where do we begin? How do we prepare for it?

As a start, I want to introduce a few key directions.

RECOGNIZE AND COMMISSION THE MARKETPLACE APOSTLES

Leadership in the marketplace or workplace, especially those in the business and corporate sectors, must be engaged. When leaders are commissioned and recognized as ministers in the marketplace, they will begin to recognize their value for kingdom purposes. The people to be reached are beyond the church walls. The systems and institutions to be changed are also beyond the church walls. The role and scope of marketplace apostles and their influence is far reaching and more powerful than we think. Fivefold ministries should commission marketplace leaders in their midst with prophetic words and prayers, sending them forth to their respective spheres of influence. God can use them powerfully to establish His kingdom in their respective areas of calling and to transform nations.

TRAIN AND EQUIP THE MARKETPLACE APOSTLES

To be effective in ministering to people, the right character ingredients must be instilled into the leaders. This is even more crucial when you engage with people who do not believe in God or His purposes. Marketplace apostles can serve with distinction or be very successful in business or work, but maintaining a good attitude of humility and respect for those in authority is equally important.

At the same time, apostles need to know how to walk close to God and be able to operate in the gifts of the Spirit, exercising the prophetic gifts with full anointing when the need arises. Spiritual gifts such as discernment, word of knowledge, and healing should never be confined to within the church walls. The gifts of the Spirit can be exercised even in the marketplace, in our jobs, services, and in our immediate places of influence.

WORK TOGETHER WITH THE YOUNG GENERATION

A new generation with substance must be raised up like Daniel, Joseph, Nehemiah, and Esther. Instill in them a right vision, a sense of destiny and purpose for their lives. Put the right attitude and values in them at a young age. Teach them to excel and persevere through suffering.

Let us work alongside the younger generation and stand by them to see nation transformation in their generation. Do not ever think that time has passed by the older generation and consider it a closed chapter. Let the father's generation link up with the sons, strengthen them, and impart to them our wisdom, values, and experiences to cause this coming generation to be groomed for success and confidence in the Lord. God can raise them up to step into roles of influence to fulfill His purposes and destiny for the nation.

We are not just talking about one or two, but a generation numbering hundreds of thousands of potential "nation transformers" in various areas of influence. But remember, it has to start with us, now, as parents, spiritual parents, teachers, instructors, mentors, and coaches. How far the younger ones make it will be determined by how much we input into their lives.

Joy Dawson and her husband, Jim, raised up their son John Dawson, who wrote *Taking Our Cities for God: How to Break Spiritual Strongholds.* His book, written in 1989, became a watershed in taking cities for God through identificational repentance, humbling ourselves, and intercession.

Network with Spiritual Fathers and Link with Intercessors

For the more immediate, short-term goal, it is crucial for the fathers of the nations to link up and come to a common ground for goals, both nationally and regionally, over a city or community. Something powerful can happen when spiritual fathers of the land recognize their roles and take up their positions as gatekeepers, to provide leadership and covering for intercessors.

What is God saying about our present times? What is the strategy to transform our city, community, and nation? We need to link up with the intercessors and the prophets and corporately hear the cry from heaven and what God would have us do. Let us learn to develop a network linking the fathers of the nation with the prophetic and intercessory people in a strong relationship. Meeting regularly as a corporate body to pray, seek God regarding the next moves, and stand in the gap for our city, community, region, and nation is a good tactic.

In Malaysia, the National Leaders Gathering (now known as Family

Journey Malaysia, following the Canadian model of David Demian) is an assembly of spiritual fathers and intercessors to pray and intercede for the nation with the desire to see Malaysia fulfill her God-given destiny. This prayer network has been active for a number of years, and we have gone to various states and cities for prayer assignments.

Another prayer movement bringing intercessors, leaders, and pastors from various churches nationally is MNPN, the Malaysian National Prayer Network. This movement is also important because mainline denominations such as Methodist, Presbyterian, and Anglican are all well represented. They are taking praying for the nation seriously and encouraging every Christian to pray for the nation at noon each day. The pastors meet weekly and have a yearly conference.

Every year, the National Evangelical Christian Fellowship (NECF Malaysia), the association for all evangelical churches in Malaysia, holds a forty-day prayer and fasting one meal a day to pray for the nation and church. I attended the recent launch of their 40-Day Annual Prayer and Fasting on August 2, 2011, held at the SIB Church, along with several other council members to represent the NECF Malaysia as a council member and lead in prayer for the economy of Malaysia. It was encouraging to see more than fifty pastors join with their intercessors to pray for the nation. I was struck when Pastor Lee Choo of SIB Church remarked that leaders are to get out together with the intercessors to pray and have a prayer drive because they bring spiritual authority, especially in dealing with strongholds. Her statement carries a vital principle of doing spiritual warfare.

When spiritual warfare teams were formed for evangelical churches in the Central Region of Malaysia, capital and training were given for spiritual mapping and principles of spiritual warfare in 2010. The pastors and leaders of the participating churches were given specific instructions to lead their teams to their allocated assignments because they carry spiritual authority for doing spiritual warfare.

1. Some twenty years ago, at a time when there was a lot of emphasis on the prayer movement and intercession, intercessors played a leading role in bringing about revival. They practiced spiritual warfare over an area or cities and covered their nations with prayers. Peter Wagner and Cindy Jacobs

were at the forefront of this movement, and I was also part of the Southeast Asia's Spiritual Warfare Network under the AD2000 Movement.

2. We have seen how intercessors play a major role in bringing forth reconciliation rather than violence in South Africa and other countries within the 10/40 window, the region between 10 and 40 degrees north of the equator that is known to have the least access to the Christian message in the world. Roughly two-thirds of the world population lives in this region, and it is primarily populated by people who are Muslim, Buddhist, animist, Jewish, or atheist. Many governments in the 10/40 window are formally or informally opposed to Christian work of any kind within their borders.

3. Even though AD2000 ceased to exist by the year 2000, many other prayer movements continued to influence and create an impact in various nations. As we begin to move into the twenty-first century, there has been a restoration of apostles and a new recognition and release of their ministries.

4. Since its early days, I was privileged to be part of this movement initiated by C. Peter Wagner and learned much, especially through my involvement with the Apostolic Roundtable, a group of about twenty-four apostles who met together annually. The Apostolic Roundtable was discontinued when C. Peter Wagner formed the International Coalition of Apostles (ICA), serving as the presiding apostle and passing the presiding mantle to Apostle John Kelly in 2011. Presently called ICAL, the International Coalition of Apostolic Leaders is one of the most strategic apostolic networks in the world and has thousands of members in more than sixty nations.[3]

Redeem the missing link

With the release of apostles taking place, people are beginning to recognize the spiritual authority carried by apostles. The term *authority* can at times be rather controversial in certain segments of the church. Therefore, some prefer to use the term *fathers of the land*. A majority of these apostles are senior pastors of large churches or are heading a network of churches. Even though all of them are supportive of the intercessory ministry, not many play a leading role. But a shift is taking place. It is the apostles or fathers of the nation or land that come together to pray and lead intercession and prayer for the nations. While the involvement of intercessors is still crucial, when these *fathers* take the lead, the impact is so much greater as they release greater authority over the nations.

We are coming to a time of greater potential impact, when the fathers of the land or apostles are taking the lead linked hand-in-hand with the intercessors.

Many of us noticed that the prayer and intercessory movements did not cause a major transformation of cities over a period of at least fifteen years. Actually, the nation of Argentina went down in terms of its economy in spite of fifteen years of revival and great prayer and intercession.

When compared to Guatemala, there was a noticeable difference. During a meeting of the Apostolic Roundtable in Colorado Springs in early 2000 (which my wife and I attended, as I was a member of the Apostolic Round-table), Harold Caballeros shared his analysis comparing Guatemala and Argentina, concluding that Guatemala was transformed because it was led by apostles, while Argentina suffered an economic downturn and was not transformed because it was led by pastors. Little wonder that a significant percentage of the Guatemalan population adhere to Christianity. In recent years, growth among the ethnic Mayans has been particularly strong. Christians are also creating an impact in various spheres of influence in culture, including education.

In the past, when the intercessors took the lead in spearheading new movements, it often resulted in clashes with their senior pastors, causing many emotional casualties. Thus, many intercessors moved out and started their own prayer ministries. Pastors were often hurt, and some felt that the good people had been drained out of the churches to join these groups.

We need to redeem this missing link between fathers and intercessors. We are coming to a time of greater potential impact, when the fathers of the land or apostles are taking the lead linked hand-in-hand with the intercessors. We will see a deeper impact and change in the spiritual realm as well as in the natural when this happens. When apostles and intercessors learn to work as a team, it becomes a powerful combination.

The Watchmen for the Nations: the Canadian journey

The Watchmen for the Nations movement is an excellent example of the apostolic and intercessory move that has shifted a nation. It was started by Pastor Bob Birch in 1991. David Demian, his spiritual son, took over the helm, and in 1994 he received a prophetic word to have a conference. The outcome was a gathering held in Whistler, British Columbia, Canada, with 2,300 people coming together to wait upon the Lord. From this meeting, the First Nations people had a leading in their hearts to take rightful stewardship over the land and repent of idolatry. The following July, another gathering took place in Victoria, British Columbia, which was marked by a time of repentance to reconcile the fathers to the children. These two gatherings were only the beginning of what God was doing. God's promises remained unfulfilled, and warnings of judgment increased.[4]

In September 1997, David was shown by the Spirit of the Lord that Canada's history of anti-Semitism had to be dealt with. One incident in particular concerned the *SS St. Louis*, a ship that carried nine hundred German Jews fleeing persecution during World War II that was denied entry into Canada. Eventually the ship returned to Europe, and this resulted in 25 percent of the passengers dying in concentration camps.[5] David and his associate pastor, Gideon Chiu, then traveled throughout Canada to share what God had revealed to them. As a result, the leaders of Christian ministries all over Canada agreed that they had put their finger on this significant root issue.

In November 1998, a gathering took place where more than six hundred leaders and intercessors came together to weep and travail before the Lord. David also traveled and appeared on television to issue a call to believers to gather in Winnipeg between June 30 and July 2, 1999, for a time of national repentance. Twenty-three hundred Canadians attended that gathering during the Canada Day weekend, which was broadcast live for four hours by satellite over the nation. After this event, many felt that they had crossed a threshold from a place of judgment to a place of favor.

In 2000, the survivors of the *SS St. Louis* were invited to Canada, where

Canadian church leaders repented for the wrongdoings. This was followed by 550 Canadians traveling to Israel in May 2001 to repent of anti-Semitism and inaction during the Holocaust. They went to Chief Rabbi Yisrael Meir Lau at the Holocaust Memorial and to Deputy Minister of Foreign Affairs Rabbi Michael Melchior at the Knesset. Other trips and dialogues took place between these two nations that further developed mutual trust and love.

Another issue to be dealt with was the divide between French and English Canadians. During the Kelowna gathering in September 2001, English and French leaders from Canada came together for reconciliation. Then in August 2002, at the birthplace of the Confederation at Charlottetown, Prince Edward Island, in front of 1,500 Canadian believers, French and English Canadian church leaders prophetically agreed to court one another for the "impending marriage," a term that the first prime minister of Canada, Sir John A. Macdonald, and the fathers of the Confederation frequently used to describe the formation. This courtship took place in the form of the La Danse Celebration Tour, from July 23 to August 9, 2003. A team of 250 toured twelve cities, where they were received with celebration services and artistic expressions of the city's unique redemptive gifts and culture.

During this time, the Watchmen held a number of leadership meetings with a desire to see unity as Jesus prayed in John 17. A major step in this journey took place at a National Leadership Gathering held in Kelowna, September 18–20, 2001. Leaders died to their own agenda and set goals to live for each other. One hundred and ten leaders performed a prophetic act by each taking a stick, binding them together, and setting them alight in a covenant of unity. (See Ezekiel 37.)

Many other meetings followed in 2002 and 2003, where the hearts of leaders were knitted together and their covenant with one another deepened. In March 2004, at the Ottawa Gathering, a cluster of leadership was formed, comprising leaders from every region of Canada, not through organization but through relationship.

The leaders of Watchmen for the Nations believed that Canada would be a model of how God can heal a nation. The great transformation of the government took place after the May 2, 2011, election, where the Conservative Party, with a significant percentage of Christian members of Parliament, won by a slim majority—less than 40 percent of the vote. Liberals lost more than half of their seats, making the New Democrats the official opposition.

In addition, the separatist party of Quebec lost 90 percent of its seats and was virtually eliminated from Parliament. As a result of this election, no party held the majority in the House of Commons for seven years.[6]

Since 2001, the Lord has opened doors for the leaders of the Watchmen on the Wall Ministries to minister in other nations, including Taiwan, Switzerland, and Germany. Today, many other countries have expressed their interest to walk this way to transform their nations, such as Hong Kong, South Africa, Singapore, Malaysia, South Korea, and many others.

Overcoming the problem: independence vs. insecurity

As the gathering of fathers of the nations took place, I came across a good number of intercessors in Malaysia who loved God and were fully focused on their intercessory ministries but had left their churches, deeply hurt from not being accepted or covered by their pastors. At countless meetings with intercessors I have stood in the gap to represent a number of pastors who have led these intercessors, and asked for forgiveness from the intercessors and at the same time received their responses.

One of the reasons why intercessors leave is because they do not fully understand the important spiritual principle of having the covering of a father in spiritual warfare. At the same time, most pastors and senior pastors shrink back from taking the lead in the prayer movement because they feel it is more convenient to leave it to the intercessors to take the lead for this function. Whatever the intercessors received from God through revelation and intercession, the pastors did not seem responsive of, excited about, or willing to take responsibility for. As a result, intercessors have felt slighted and unsupported in their role. On the other hand, some pastors have believed that intercessors have crossed the line of authority from being enthusiastic to being detrimental to the life of the church. These intercessors would rather listen to God than the authority of the pastors. I have heard from many pastors about how hurt they were by the intercessors that have left their churches.

However, intercessors have a valuable gifting and important role in the kingdom of God. They carry the intense burden to cry out to the Lord and birth God's move for the nation. Many of them are prophetic, some are also prophets, and they also receive revelation. At the same time, they need the leadership of the apostles to give them spiritual covering and guidance.

The time for reconciliation is now, and the need is great. If only we can all see the big picture together!

There is a spiritual vacuum to fill for fathers of the land. Spiritual fathers need to step up and take the lead, giving covering to all these intercessors. Senior pastors need to provide leadership and covering for intercessors and be involved in the prayer movement, whether within the church or in an interchurch movement. Both intercessors and apostles need to recognize each other's roles.

A new synergistic move can take the church to greater dimensions of victory. Apostolic fathers praying and taking the lead while linking up with intercessors will see the advancement of the kingdom of God.

ENGAGE WITH GOVERNMENT

Engage and interact with the government. This was a concept considered to be virtually taboo for many churches in the past. But engage we must. It is essential for us to do so if we want to see changes in the nation.

We must relate to our nation and guard its future. Whether it is the local council, city council, elected representatives over the states, or those in federal government, we as the church cannot afford to run away from this responsibility. Stand by the people and statesmen as they serve, and pray with them in the course of nation building. Encourage Christians to work jointly with them toward achieving good governance, and support them in their fight against corruption, poverty, and injustice. Engage with the legislature as well, because they do a vital job in terms of getting laws passed. Pray and stand with them, and encourage and affirm them that they are doing a great purpose to fulfill the destiny of our nation. It can be a very lonely struggle that these people go through. There are many battles and issues they need to face. Just like any of us, they also need to be encouraged and affirmed that they are playing a vital role.

Pray for the judiciary as well, that all the magistrates and judges will be good men and women who are righteous and just. Young people must be encouraged to study law, and have the desire and aspirations to someday be magistrates and judges in our nations so that God's righteous justice will prevail over the land. If we do not engage in these areas now or encourage a new generation of young people to aspire to such positions, we will never see godly people being placed in such positions to change the system.

Something powerful can happen when spiritual fathers of the land recognize their roles and take up their positions as gatekeepers, to provide leadership and covering for intercessors.

Work with Businesspeople toward Transference of Wealth

To see nation transformation and the transference of wealth taking place, we must learn to work with those in the marketplace, especially those in businesses. Financial wealth provides the means to finance kingdom projects and eradicate poverty, build infrastructure, create jobs, provide loans, and feed the poor—not just in our nation but also for other nations of the world, including third-world countries.

As of 2006, in Southeast Asia alone there were many countries with high levels of poverty, including Cambodia (with 78 percent living below the poverty line), Laos (74 percent), Myanmar (23 percent), Indonesia (52 percent), and the Philippines (48 percent). By sheer population alone, a huge amount of people are in poverty in India (80 percent), Bangladesh (83 percent), Pakistan (74 percent), Nepal (69 percent), and even China (47 percent), not to mention the countries of Africa. With China at 1.3 billion and India at 1.1 billion, both these nations make up more than one-third of the world's total population of 6.6 billion. Just in China and India alone there were an estimated 1.5 billion people living below the poverty line in 2006.[7]

Since 2006, situations have greatly improved. Recent statistics show that the poverty rate in the Philippines has gone down to 25.8 percent,[8] indicating that the nation is in the process of being transformed by the power of God.

We can work with the marketplace leaders to:

+ Identify God's kingdom purpose for them to achieve in their sphere of influence.

+ Strategize with them about ways for the body of Christ to help support them in extending the kingdom of God within their sphere of influence in the marketplace.

+ Connect with and support the Joseph and Daniel types of marketplace leaders who have prophetic and revelational insights.

+ Develop models for individuals and churches that want to develop businesses in nations as a nation transformation effort. If possible, help them publicize and connect with the right individuals to achieve that goal.

+ Partner with business leaders in bringing new business and job prospects to nations that are closed to ministries but open for businesses.

WHAT MUST THE CHURCH DO TO FACILITATE NATION TRANSFORMATION?

1. Establish the government of God and His authority over cities, communities, regions, and nations.

Recognition of apostles and their roles

Apostles hold divine authority over nations, people groups, and cities. When they come together with a spirit of unity, they carry God's spiritual authority over the nation. Corporately, they can hear what God is saying. This is known as "corporate hearing." Until and unless the church recognizes this aspect, positions and authority cannot be aligned for kingdom purposes. Apostles carry divine authority to make decrees and proclamations, such as those made over the Philippines in 2007.

Apostles not only make decrees but they can also give spiritual covering to prophets, intercessors, and spiritual sons. Apostles receive strategies for nation transformation in various spheres of society—in government, business, media, and education. They can seek God's strategy for the best way to move.

The Australian Coalition of Apostles was initiated through Peter Wagner's visit to Canberra in October 2009. John MacNamara, a member of the International Coalition of Apostles, called for the first meeting, and I was privileged to be invited to join. I also attended the second meeting on

February 17, 2010, which received endorsement from those of us who were present and all contributed to discussion about its values, vision, mission statement, and its executive council. During the lunch break, John MacNamara requested that several apostles pray for Zed Seselja, the opposition leader (Liberals) of Australian Capital Territory (ACT). It was also heartwarming to hear Jim Wallace, managing director of the Australian Christian Lobby, share the vision of the Australian Coalition of Apostles.

Many pastors have not yet accepted the idea of apostles in the marketplace and usually do not endorse them. These workplace apostles who run businesses are anointed by God, prophetically and apostolically, and will also naturally plant churches. If God's nuclear church leaders refuse change, God will always have His alternatives. Look at Nehemiah, a mere cupbearer with no nation-building qualifications whatsoever. God bypassed the rest and chose cupbearer Nehemiah to rebuild the city of Jerusalem. God is interested in using only the willing. When people refuse to listen, He will use other means. We need to wake up and realize that ultimately it is what God wants that matters—nothing else.

Daniel 7:9–10 mentions thrones set in place as the Ancient of Days takes His seat. What are the thrones to be set in place for God to take His position? When God's fivefold ministries are aligned to take up their positions as His government, then God's rulership can be established. There is a spiritual order on earth coming together with a spirit of humility and servanthood as they align themselves with God's purposes and will. As a result, the courts of heaven will gain authority over a particular situation, region, church, or nation. Only then can God release His judgment and transform these areas. God may change or reshuffle the leadership of the nation. He can tear down or build up power structures, giving power to whomever He wills, pulling down every dictator and arrogant leader. The decree of the court of heaven always favors the saints of God. He can turn the tide against the enemy.

> As I watched, this horn was waging war against the holy people and defeating them, until the Ancient of Days came and pronounced judgment in favor of the holy people of the Most High, and the time came when they possessed the kingdom.
>
> —Daniel 7:21–22, niv

This is what will happen if God's fivefold ministry in an area or nation can be united. However, if God's people fail to unite and take their place in God's apostolic government, He will creatively release the new wineskin, the coalition of the willing.

Not everyone will agree at first, and the excitement of what God is doing may only hit a handful, yet God can establish a new wineskin and structure to fulfill His purposes. By the term *structure*, I don't just mean a nuclear church. It can be in the marketplace too. At first, a small group of like-minded people may seem insignificant, but as the fivefold ministry begins to function and grow, God's government will also be established.

Beyond just another fellowship

An apostolic council is involved with a city, region, or nation, and comprises both marketplace and nuclear church apostles. Although a pastors' fellowship that provides fellowship, sharing, and praying over needs is good for strengthening and encouraging, an apostolic network or council is set up for the purpose of transforming a city, region, or nation.

Some people may think, *Why come together when we can't even agree on our theologies and doctrinal stand?* Coming together for city transformation calls for all to gather in humbleness, putting aside our personal agendas in order to seek God and fulfill His purposes alone. It does not mean changing each other's perspectives and practices. What is most important is that God knits our hearts together by the Spirit. As we allow God to link our hearts together by covenant relationship, we are united in spirit, and John 17 can become a reality:

> I have given them the glory that you gave me, that they may be one as we are one—I in them and you in me—so that they may be brought to complete unity. Then the world will know that you sent me and have loved them even as you have loved me.
>
> —JOHN 17:22–23, NIV

This is not a unity where we just find some common issue to agree on but still do not want to get too close for comfort or even step into each other's churches. God seeks the kind of unity where bonding takes place in love and trust for each other even if we have just met.

Once, during one of the Malaysia fathers' gatherings held in Penang, the head of the network in Penang invited me to preach at his church, and I agreed. Both of us have the same mind-set of preferring to preach at our own churches rather than at other people's churches. However, this was an unusual occasion, because I ended up preaching at his church one Sunday, and later he came to preach at our church too. God can knit us in the Spirit so strongly that nothing can break the bond. Truly the Spirit can bind hearts and make people *click* beyond comprehension.

2. *The church should engage with the marketplace through marketplace apostles.*

a. Educate and shift the mind-sets of our congregation from stained glass to marketplace. (See chapter 3.)

Ministry should not be confined within the four walls of the church alone. We must recognize that those in the marketplace are also ministers. Even Naaman's young maid influenced her master to seek healing in Israel. As a result, the master returned with two bags of soil, indicating that he wanted to return to worship the God of Israel. If she, a mere maid, can be such a great influence, how much more can you be used by God? Wherever you work, you can influence those in authority as they observe your life.

b. Provide avenues for marketplace apostles to meet and network in their cities, regions, or nations.

A church leader from the Philippines who considers me as his spiritual father came to Malaysia to observe the Kingdom Club, and he went back to form the Kingdom Circle so that businesspeople and government leaders could meet together. Now they have fifty-two churches coming together with joined hearts, including meeting with businesspeople and leaders in local government once a month. They also avail their premises for kingdom purposes, training, and conferences. They are making an impact in the city of Mandaluyong, part of the Manila metro area, through their monthly programs and events.

The Kingdom Club in Malaysia hosted a seminar in a hotel for Hope Taylor of the International Leadership Embassy. Several leading politicians attended in addition to businesspeople. One businessman who runs a carpet factory faced business crisis when his factory was running at a loss. After he joined the Kingdom Club in Malaysia, intercession and prayers were made for him and his factory business. A team was sent to pray and to anoint his factory with oil, and within two years he was making a good profit.

Recently, this man singlehandedly contributed almost the total amount needed for the building of an indigenous church building in Sarawak near the Indonesian border. (The intention of the gatherings is not to solicit contributions; however, businesspeople are often blessed and want to contribute where they are seeing the kingdom of God going forward.) A team from Kingdom Club joined me to attend the opening and dedication ceremony of the church, where more than two hundred people attended, including community leaders and headmen from surrounding villages.

Mission teams were sent to Indonesia, Cambodia, and Sarawak, and they made an impact on the churches through involvement in ministry of teaching, preaching, praying for the needy, and practical ministry like offering to build a barbecue set for the church to use in their ministry to young people. This was in addition to financial contributions.

> c. Commission, anoint and release the marketplace apostles before the congregation.

When I was in Australia, I asked Peter Young, one of the councilors of Gold Coast, to come over so that we could release and anoint him. We drew close to him because when he exposed corruption within government circles, he was charged with defamation and almost went bankrupt. Though he was not able to rally strong support and encouragement from local churches (except his local church, with his pastor offering strong support), I was convinced that God's people should stand by him. I knew that if we brought people together to stand alongside and minister to him, God could turn things around for him and strengthen his will to persevere. Alongside businesspeople and several pastors, I commissioned and released him to his role in the Gold Coast to work for the city with the mayor. We prophesied over the city that it would be an international city, a blueprint model of what God can do to turn things around.

Not long after that, Peter ran again for councilor in the election in 2008 and won by a landslide. His legal case was settled through an out-of-court settlement, thus enabling him to move forward. In 2012 he ran for mayor in the local election, and though he did not win, God has a better plan for him. God is working in his life and heart toward this goal. He knew that one section of their society, the developers, would be crucial. His challenge was to change the perception of the developers, who believed him to be anti-developers and anti-development, and to show that he was in favor of sustained and balanced development in the city.

In November 2009, the city councilor was chairing the committee with the responsibility of a leading developer's huge development project in the city. However, since there had been personal animosity between the councilor and this particular developer over the years, it looked like the developer's bid would be rejected, and that meant he would face financial turmoil. Instead of rejecting the bid as a form of retaliation, this councilor spoke convincingly for this developer's project, and the Council approved it with favorable terms. The developer was overwhelmed and wrote a heartfelt letter of thanks to the councilor. What a change of heart; what a testimony for the Lord!

> d. Let the fivefold ministries—apostles, prophets, evangelists, pastors, and teachers—stand with the marketplace apostles when they face challenges in the workplace, and pray until answers come.

Intercessors play a key role in keeping watch over events and other critical developments unfolding in the nation, as government servants need constant covering and prayers in upholding righteousness and justice in the system. Teachers and evangelists can help train, equip, and reach out to key individuals who seek to know God. Prophets can help sense the direction of events and see God's purposes for them.

One of the most effective ways to come alongside workplace apostles is to relate with government servants personally and set time to share with them God-given insights, prophetic words, and counsel, and to pray for each one individually (preferably in their homes, workplaces, or in a private setting).

Secondly, explore ways in which the church can contribute to the development of the communities they represent. Elected state representatives from various political parties requested church participation in the cleaning up of certain areas of their communities; others requested for volunteers to count votes.

3. The church should engage with the government.

Our role is not to condemn or criticize but to intercede, pray, share prophetic insights, and give godly counsel with a spirit of humility. Normally when the church approaches the government, it is primarily to ask for favor, help, or aid. However, we need to change this attitude; when we meet government and political leaders, our primary objective should be to stand alongside them to assist them. We are to offer to pray for them—the congressmen, senators, judges, cabinet ministers, mayors, governors, and city councilors.

Do not ignore or avoid contact with government leaders anymore. Their need for support and prayers is real, as they face various challenges, issues to resolve, and temptations, and they need to make critical decisions that may result in good or even bad ramifications.

4. Fathers or senior ministers should link with the "sons."

We cannot accomplish what is necessary without linking with the "sons" generation.

> Behold, I will send you Elijah the prophet before the coming of the great and dreadful day of the LORD. And he will turn the hearts of the fathers to the children, and the hearts of the children to their fathers, lest I come and smite the earth with a curse.
>
> —MALACHI 4:5–6, NIV

When three generations come together to fulfill God's purposes, the outcome will be very powerful. Believe in the younger generation of leaders. Raise them up and stand by them so that they can see the fulfillment of God's purposes and destiny for their nation. Inspire and challenge the younger generation to acquire the best education and training possible in order to be positioned in many different areas of influence.

During Daniel's time, he was ten times better than the average scholar! Make sure that our sons are raised up ten times better than the average person. Grant them godly wisdom, anointing, prophetic insight, and all the dynamics of spiritual ministry. Challenge them to make a commitment like Daniel did. He did not defile himself when in office but became the vehicle of God to fulfill His purposes. In Daniel 1:8, we see that Daniel committed himself to not be defiled when he was still young. When entering the place of office or influence with a commitment before God, Daniel was not corrupted.

Godly leaders will not be motivated by wealth or position because of the constant awareness that God's hand is upon them.

In the Philippines, young children receive prophecies that they will move into studying law and make the best attempt possible to go to Harvard, Yale, and other top universities because this will enable them to take up influential positions in government and the judiciary. Some of them want to be president and to be in top government positions to help turn the nation around. Looking at their faces, I know they are serious. Wholeheartedly they give themselves to the Lord, fully involved in ministry. At the same time, they put their hearts into their studies and constantly excel. Let the pastors and church leaders and their parents do the same to challenge their young children.

The change starts *now*. For the long-term, let us start to raise up at least three to four generations of leaders for our nations. How we respond will determine the outcome of our nations in future years.

CHAPTER 9
CONVERGENCE

*S*HALL A NATION be born in a day?

> Who has heard such a thing? Who has seen such things? Shall the
> earth be made to give birth in one day? Or shall a nation be born
> at once?
>
> —ISAIAH 66:8

Rapid gatherings of leaders and intercessors shift nations so quickly that
the transformation process accelerates.

CONNECTING PRINCIPLES OF SPIRITUAL WARFARE WITH APOSTOLIC AND PROPHETIC LEADERSHIP

Working together to transform culture and to reform laws and structures
based on a biblical worldview results in real transformation and change for
a nation.

Cindy Jacobs said it correctly: "If we transform without putting reformational laws, structures, and a biblical worldview into our everyday lives,
society will revert to its former state."[1] Cindy further defines reformation as
"an amendment or repair of what is corrupt, to build the institutions of our
governments and society according to their God-ordained order and organization. It means to institutionalize God's will in how we do our daily business, deal with the poor, administer justice, make our laws, teach our children,
and generally live our lives. It is to give people a license to do good and not
a license to sin. It means turning our communities into places where God's
blessings flow from person to person just as God sees them flow in heaven."[2]

In my more than ten years of observation and involvement in the transformation of cities, communities, and nations, I have witnessed both failures
and successes. The year 2014 was a pivotal year for me in relation to finishing
my book. I was reconnected to the Family Journey of David Demian and
Gideon Chiu, and I joined them in numerous meetings both in Malaysia
and Jerusalem. In October of 2014 I was able to participate at the annual

meeting of the Heartland Apostolic Prayer Network (HAPN) in Oklahoma City with Apostle John Benefiel leading. I went to the Philippines twice in 2014 and participated in the "Touching Heaven, Changing Earth" conference in Dipolog City, and reconnected with the rapid transformation taking place in the Philippines. My trip to Canberra, Adelaide, and Melbourne in that year played a part in the latest movement for the transformation of Australia.

We need to look at models that work and identify roadmaps to the transformation. The convergence of applying spiritual warfare principles and apostles and prophets coming together with strategic persons that God has raised up and used results in transformation of nations. Three outstanding models that have proven to be successful, and with which I have been involved, are the following:

+ HAPN of John Benefiel, based in Oklahoma City
+ Family Journey of David Demian and Gideon Chiu, based in Vancouver, Canada
+ Transformation of the nation of the Philippines

HAPN (Heartland Apostolic Prayer Network)

Led by Apostle John Benefiel, HAPN is built upon the foundations laid by the Spiritual Warfare Movement led by C. Peter Wagner and the team of outstanding leaders including Cindy Jacobs, Barbara Wentroble, Chuck Pierce, George Otis Jr., Doris Wagner, and several others. I was with them as one of the founding members around 1986. In 2001, after the Spiritual Warfare Network ended under the AD2000 Movement, C. Peter Wagner convened the Apostolic Roundtable. John Benefiel and I were part of the twenty-four apostles of the Apostolic Roundtable.

Why was HAPN effective as compared with the Spiritual Warfare Network?

One of the discussions was that after fifteen years of spiritual warfare under the Spiritual Warfare Network and AD2000 Movement, though it was a great blessing to the nations in the 10/40 window, not a single city or nation was transformed through spiritual warfare alone. The component that was missing was the apostles taking leadership in spiritual warfare networks in the nations and not merely leaving that task to intercessors and pastors.

Prophets need to work alongside apostles, as Chuck Pierce, a prophet, works hand in hand with Apostle John Benefiel.

In 1995, Chuck Pierce, one of the most strategic prophets over cities and nations, sensed something was wrong. He sensed something foreboding in the atmosphere in Oklahoma City a week before the Oklahoma City bombing at the Alfred P. Murrah Federal Building. John Benefiel rose "as a leader to mobilize leaders, encourage intercession, become a change agent, and create a model that would change the course of a city, a state, and a nation."[3]

HAPN applied principles of spiritual warfare thoroughly. They learned from George Otis Jr. about spiritual mapping, and they did exactly that. They also learned from him about four major iniquities that had to be dealt with: immorality, idolatry, broken covenants, and innocent bloodshed—they were convinced that Oklahoma had them all. They were inspired by George Otis's *Transformation* video about cities transformed, especially encouraged by the transformation of Almolonga, a community of twenty thousand in Guatemala. They became aware that one of the most important components for the transformation of a city is persevering leadership.

What are some of the special experiences of the Oklahoma City Prayer Network that we can learn from?

1. "First and foremost, God instructed us to heal the divisions in the Body of Christ and allow Him to establish the government of the church in our cities and state. This involved repentance and reconciliation with groups that had been made to feel inferior, like dishonored and unwanted members of the Body of Christ. God expected us to cross denominational and racial barriers, especially with African American and Native American believers."[4]

    It was not simply saying "I'm sorry," but establishing the kind of covenantal relationship that meant they would be willing to lay their lives down for one another.

2. Learn that there is no statute of limitations for sin and iniquity. That means spiritual darkness can linger here because of the unrepented sins of our ancestors. "Those iniquities defiled the land and allowed demonic strongholds to blind the eyes

of unbelievers to the gospel. It created a mountain of spiritual darkness that resisted genuine change in every area of our culture: churches, families, education, government, arts and entertainment, media and communications, and the marketplace."[5]

3. They heard and obeyed the words of the prophets—first Chuck Pierce, then Cindy Jacobs, Barbara Wentroble, and others. "One of the prophetic words spoken over Oklahoma by Cindy Jacobs was, 'If Oklahoma is OK, the nation will be OK.' And 'As Oklahoma goes, so goes the nation.'"[6]

4. They dealt with the broken covenant between the United States and the Native Americans. One covenant Joshua made with the Gibeonites centuries ago and broken by Saul brought about God's judgement in the form of famine for three years until amends could be made. David carried out the Gibeonites' request, and after that God answered their prayer on behalf of the land (2 Sam. 21:14). John Benefiel stated that from the year 1778 until 1883, the United States government negotiated but the treaties were never ratified, although some took legal effect. All of them were broken.[7]

5. The Baal Divorce Decree—Dutch Sheets taught in 2007 that the god of America is Baal. Apostle Jerry Marsh was asked by John Benefiel to write a decree of divorce. In corporate meetings of leaders and intercessors from across the state, the petition of divorce was taken before the highest court in the kingdom of God. This was where they officially divorced Baal and renounced all the fruit of that union. After that, they officially married the Lord Jesus, thus renewing their covenant with Him. (The Baal Divorce Decree can be found in John Benefiel's book *Binding the Strongman over America*, Appendix A.)

6. Tangible and measurable results—C. Peter Wagner considers HAPN to have "the most tangible, measurable results of high-level prayer and spiritual warfare that I have heard yet in my life."[8]

John Benefiel says:

> Fifteen years ago, Oklahoma City was so spiritually disjointed that
> when God sent a prophet to warn us of impending doom, he could
> find no cohesive group to tell. The bombing in downtown Oklahoma
> City left it deserted, and looking like a war zone. Our economy had
> long suffered as Oklahoma stood at the back of the class in most
> areas of our society. There was nothing here to draw people or
> businesses.
>
> Today, the church in Oklahoma City is strong, and Christian
> leaders have taken their place in Church government. We have
> leaders in each region, and meet together on a regular basis to pray.
> If that weren't enough, God has established our efforts as a model
> for the nation...
>
> While the nation is in the middle of a high recession and wide-
> scale unemployment, Forbes magazine listed Oklahoma City as the
> No. 1 most recession-proof city in the nation.[9]

In November 2004, for the first time since statehood, the House of Representatives was won by conservative Christians. In 2008, both the House
and the Senate were controlled by conservative Christians. As a result, good
laws have been passed in Oklahoma since 2004.

During the HAPN conference in October 2014, repentance was made for
the GOP, the Republican Party, as research indicated corruption took place
in the party in earlier days involving oil money in a hotel meeting in Chicago.
Could there be a correlation to the midterm election victory on November 4,
2014, for the Republicans for both Houses—Senate and Congress—and an
increase in governorships across the nation? John Benefiel believed that was
the case.

After prayers were offered that changed the state legislature and executive branch in 2004, 2006, 2008, and 2010, the following laws were passed:[10]

+ Constitutional amendment defining marriage as between one
  man and one woman
+ Civil justice reform
+ Increased penalty for possession of child pornography
+ Anti-abortion laws:

2007: No state funds, employees, or facilities may be used for abortions

2008: Protection for healthcare providers refusing to participate; regulates use of dangerous chemical pill RU-486; ensures mother's consent to abort is truly voluntary; provides a woman with an ultrasound of her unborn child prior to undergoing the abortion; bans wrongful-life lawsuits that claim a baby would have been better off aborted.

2009: Allows a pregnant woman to use deadly force to protect her unborn child; bans abortions based on the sex of a child; requires all physicians to report information about women seeking abortions or medical care after an abortion; makes it a misdemeanor to attempt to clone humans

2011: Requires abortion providers to determine the age of the fetus prior to abortion; bans abortions after twenty weeks, on the basis of fetal pain; bans insurance coverage for abortions

2012: Forty-three new restrictions enacted (second highest number of annual restrictions ever); Oklahoma leads in the total number of abortion restrictions (twenty-two restrictions) by state and category (see remappingdebate.org for more information)

According to the Associated Press, abortions in Oklahoma are down 18.7 percent from 2010 to 2013; also, according to the Americans United for Life 2016 Life List, Oklahoma is the number one pro-life state!

+ Apology Bill Passed: John Benefiel, working with Jay Swallow and Negiel Bigpond, took the initiative to meet with Senator Brownback of Kansas and submitted the Resolution of Apology into legislation. The senator introduced the bill in the Senate of the United States, and the 111th Congress passed it unanimously in 2009. The Resolution of Apology to the Native People was presented to the House of Representatives through the Indian Affairs Committee headed by Senator John McCain. The Resolution was signed into law by President Obama with the passage of the 2010 Department of Defense Appropriations Bill. The apology states, "The United States, acting through Congress...apologizes on behalf of the people of the United States to all Native Peoples for the many instances of violence, maltreatment, and neglect inflicted on Native Peoples by citizens of the United States...expresses its regret..."[11]

To date, HAPN has grown to include leaders and networks in all fifty states and forty foreign nations which are in various stages of the transformation process.

Family Journey led by David Demian and Gideon Chiu

The results and impact of the Family Journey, Asia Homecoming Gathering, One Heart—led by David Demian and Gideon Chiu of Watchmen for the Nations from Vancouver, Canada—during the last ten years have been impressive. The impact of the Family Journey in Taiwan, Hong Kong, Malaysia, and China was incredible.

The July 2013 Asia Homecoming in Hong Kong was a watershed: 16,000 participants attended the gathering, the majority of whom were from China. It was here that the spiritual representatives of the coalition of eight nations led by Britain repented and asked for forgiveness from the Chinese people for sins that were committed by their nations 170 years ago. Since that time (the First Opium War in 1839–1842; the Second Opium War in 1856–60; and finally the Peking War in 1900), the Chinese were humiliated and defeated, and unfair treaties were forced on them. The British conspired to trade with the Chinese for their goods and products with opium.

Later, the United States, France, Germany, The Netherlands, Hungary, Japan, and Portugal joined Britain in the coalition in the battle caused by the Boxer Rebellion in 1900, where churches were burned and missionaries were killed. Unfortunately this caused such strong hatred that the Chinese rejected Christianity and the gospel as Western culture and religion.[12]

Currently, this prayer and intercessory network that brings spiritual fathers and intercessors to walk together and see their nations transformed and their destiny fulfilled is making inroads into countries like Indonesia, Japan, South Korea, and Israel. Repentance was made, forgiveness was given, and reconciliation between nations represented took place. Chuck Pierce attended the conference to give to the Chinese leaders a big key, prophetic act, and said that the time for the Chinese to take the lead in preaching the pure gospel has come.

Fathers from the five underground streams of churches came and for the first time united as one family. Fathers of those movements linked with their sons, and linking the generations together as one was significant. Prior to this meeting, spiritual leaders in Taiwan were already walking in unity as one and uniting their hearts with the First Nations leaders of the native tribes. Spiritual leaders from Indonesia, Malaysia, Thailand, Japan, and many more Asian nations witnessed what took place and were stirred to see similar moves take place in their nations. The stirring to see transformation of their nations and seeing their nations fulfill God's destiny was evident.

In 2011, according to David Demian, Malaysia's Family Journey's team was instrumental in Vancouver gatherings and Hong Kong's gathering in linking the Chinese to the Middle East. The name Malaysia in Chinese means "horse" "come" "Asia West," meaning "Horse (Malaysia) come, align with Western Asia (Middle East) finally back to Jerusalem." A wooden horse that was given to David Demian as a gift arrived at the conference in Vancouver broken in four pieces. That itself carried a prophetic message, that through brokenness of hearts God will use us to fulfill His assignment.

According to David Demian, Malaysia is the joint that connects China, India, and to the Middle East.

By May 2014 there was a gathering in Jerusalem with a burden to pray for reconciliation between the Messianic and Arab pastors in which Chinese intercessors and leaders played a key role. I was a participant in this gathering where one hundred of us came from all over the world. However, half of those who attended were from China, and they came on an assignment.

One of the sons from the underground church shared the significance of their assignment to travel to Jerusalem to join us. He shared that in the years 1941 and 1942, two groups of young people independently heard the voice of God asking them to bring the gospel to Jerusalem. One group was from northern China and the other was from northeast China. Both groups took eight years to travel to the west of China, but when they arrived in 1949, the Communists had taken over and closed the door so that they could not leave China to continue their journey to Jerusalem. They had a decision to make: either go back where they came from, or wait there and pray until the door opened. They decided they would not go back, but wait and pray. They did this for more than sixty years until all of them died. Engraved on their tombstones were the words, "Kingdom Ambassadors."

The Chinese delegation had come to fulfill the assignment God had given to these two groups of young people more than seventy years earlier. Their mission was to bring reconciliation of the Messianic Jewish pastors and the Arab pastors. Though these two groups had gone through repentance and reconciliation acts many times before this season, through the Chinese brethren's passion, perseverance, and intercession, God intervened.

In the midst of the repentance and reconciliation prayers, with the Chinese brethren praying fervently, I shared the deep impression I had in my spirit: that of a thirteen-year-old lad, Ishmael, crying out to God, "My dad and my mum left me here in the wilderness to die, without food and water. What have I done wrong?" After much prayer, the Jewish brethren took turns sharing, and then the Arab brethren took turns. After all had shared, two Arab sisters—one from Nazareth and the other from Jordan—opened up their wounded hearts and spoke about their lost sense of identity and deep hurts, things that Arab brethren normally would not be able to open up about. Many wept, and the whole atmosphere shifted. We knew something significant had taken place. I had never seen such depth of identification repentance.

At the end of the sharing, I made a prophetic declaration based on Isaiah 19:23–25:

> There will be a day when there will be a highway from Egypt to Assyria—Arab nations of Syria, Lebanon, Turkey, Jordan, and Iraq. In that day, we declare Israel will be one of three with Egypt and these Arab nations, a blessing in the midst of the land, whom the Lord of hosts shall bless, saying, "Blessed is Egypt, My people [Hagar was Egyptian]; and the Arab nations of Syria, Lebanon, Turkey, and Iraq, the work of My hands; and Israel, My inheritance." Let that day come into fulfillment, in the name of Jesus. Amen.

The following month, war broke out between Hamas and Israel, and for the first time, Egypt, Saudi Arabia, and the United Arab Emirates (UAE) did not condemn Israel but rather blamed Hamas for the conflict. What we did in prayers, repentance, reconciliation, and prophetic declaration did have an effect on that war, and it looked like there was a correlation.

In December 2014, David Demian related to me that there had been two other gatherings, where more repentance and reconciliation had taken place between the Jewish and Arab brethren. These two gatherings included a large gathering of over three thousand in Jerusalem—80 percent of whom were from China—in November. Again the Chinese brethren played a crucial role, praying and interceding for the two groups.

In October, during the pregathering for the November meeting, something unprecedented took place: one Arab brother asked the Jewish brethren to "marry" (have covenant relationship, like marriage) him (representing the Arab brethren). David said that for the first time, the Jewish brethren confessed and asked forgiveness for having a racist mind-set. They loved the respect they enjoyed as elder brother but had not taken responsibility for the younger ones (implying the Arab brothers).

In September 2014, more than two thousand Japanese pastors came for a gathering in Okinawa. This was a watershed event indicating the season for harvest in Japan had come. Less than 1 percent of the Japanese population are Christians.[13]

David said he was once in a trance and saw an event of the end times. A war between two armies, one led by Christ on a white horse and the other led by the devil himself, was about to begin. As David was watching, suddenly the Lord pulled His sword and threw it into a bull's eye, a red-colored circle. After much contemplation and asking the Lord the meaning of his dream, David realized that the bull's eye was the flag of Japan. The sword was the symbol of the Japanese warring spirit as shown during World War II. The Lord told David it is the season for Japan to have harvest, and that harvest will trigger harvest across the nations of the world.

The first thing the Japanese pastors did was repent for the sins and atrocities their army had committed during World War II across numerous nations in Asia and Southeast Asia, in addition to the attack on Pearl Harbor. They believed Japan will continue living under a curse unless they stood in the gap and repented for the sins of their forefathers.

What are some special experiences of Watchmen for the Nations that we can learn from?

1. Conference call by God

David Demian wanted to see a people who are longing for the presence of God come together only because God calls them, not because of an agenda or the names of the speakers announced—"Just wait on God until He speaks to us about His heart for Canada."[14]

In 1994, Imiel Abadir, a recognized prophet from Egypt and a friend of David's, in a meeting in Vancouver with Bob Birch and David's friends in the Watchmen, began to prophesy, "There is a conference that needs to happen next year…And you have two months to plan it. If you don't start planning you will miss something. The Lord is about to do something great in your nation."[15]

2. Need to have spiritual covering of spiritual fathers and mothers

"Spiritual fathers and mothers have a very important role to play in the body of Christ by providing a spiritual covering to protect the Lord's purposes."[16]

David believed that spiritual fathers, having the benefit of experience from their journey with God, can sense obstacles in advance. At the same time they also have wisdom about how to abort the enemy's attacks before they can happen. "If younger leaders could learn to walk under the covering of trusted spiritual fathers and mothers, we could avoid a lot of 'needless casualties of war' in our pursuits for God."[17] Three spiritual fathers cover David Demian and Gideon Chiu's ministry including Bob Birch and John White.

3. Open to prophets working with them

Besides Imiel Abadir of Egypt, Chuck Pierce ministered in their gatherings in Asia Homecoming in Hong Kong in 2013, and recently in Indonesia in January 2015. On January 26 in Hong Kong, Chuck Pierce placed the whirlwind shawl on David Demian's shoulder and declared that God has anointed him as His whirlwind for Asia. David told me that Chuck did not know that he had planned a big Asian gathering in November 2015.

4. Covenant to wait on God

Watchmen make a foundational covenant that they would never initiate for God but rather they would always wait on Him until He speaks. This is the heart of their understanding of the lordship of Christ. David remarked,

"I believe that embracing death to self-rule and total surrender to His rule is the first major step in seeing the kingdom of God established."[18]

5. The challenge of hearing God

When the Lord revealed to David Demian the root issue holding back God's favor for Canada—the anti-Semitic heart of the European forefathers who founded Canada—his challenge was to call Canada to repentance or else judgment would come. In 2 Samuel 21, when David inquired of the Lord regarding the cause of three years of famine which currently beset them, the Lord replied that it was because Saul had put the Gibeonites to death and by doing so had broken the covenant Joshua made with the Gibeonites centuries earlier. As David made amends with the Gibeonites, God answered the prayer for the land (2 Sam. 21:14).

6. Corporate discernment

Corporate discernment was another foundational covenant the Watchmen made with God. It means each person tests the word from the Lord in his or her spirit, and then they come together to share what they sensed. If they cannot come to a corporate agreement, they continue to seek the Lord and talk together until they come to the place of clarity in their spirits.[19]

"As the team talked together there was a clear agreement—even if we couldn't understand logically what anti-Semitism had to do with our destiny, we felt this was something the Lord wanted us to pursue."[20] Stories came to light about Canada's anti-Semitic immigration policies during World War II. Because of these racist attitudes, many Jewish people, seeking refuge from the Nazis, were denied entry into Canada and were left to die in the gas chambers of Europe. The Lord told them that the blood of the innocent is crying out. "I want you to call Canada to repentance for its anti-Semitic heart."[21]

The story of the ship named the *SS St. Louis* surfaced. In June 1939, the *St. Louis* set sail from Germany with nine hundred Jewish people fleeing Nazi Germany to begin a new life in Cuba. Cuban authorities refused them entry for having bought fake entrance visas. Desperately they appealed to every South American country without success. Then they sailed to Miami, Florida, and sent telegrams to President Roosevelt pleading for asylum in the United States, but again the Jews were denied entry.[22]

After many weeks, they began running out of supplies. Canada was their last hope of refuge. In spite of their appeal for mercy, the Canadian Prime Minister, Mackenzie King, rejected their request. Subsequently, the ship sailed back to Germany, and after much debate, England, Belgium, The Netherlands, and France each agreed to take some refugees. The war broke out soon after, and France, Belgium, and Holland were occupied by the Nazis. More than one-third of those who had been on the ship perished in concentration camps.[23]

In my experience with this network, I was amazed at the amount of insight and revelation that was released to the Discerning Group of brothers and sisters. In 2013 the Holy Spirit revealed that God's order for Malaysia was to align the First Nation, Orang Asli or the aborigines of West Malaysia, with eighteen tribes, and the native tribes of Sarawak (forty-five tribes) and Sabah (thirty-six tribes) as the first step—like putting on the topmost button on our shirt first, then the rest will be aligned accordingly.

In the Discerning Group of February 2015, the group discerned that the capital of Sarawak, Kuching (meaning "cat" in our national language), is actually a Chinese word, Teochew dialect, meaning "ancient wells." Research shows that there were three ancient wells, and one with healing properties. Incidentally, the ancient wells were capped and locked in 1939, the year World War II broke out in Germany. Therefore, a large gathering of all tribes was planned for April 2015 in Kuching. It was revealed that Kuching is the birthplace of a significant move of God.

7. Corporate authority

Corporate authority is the result of the power of unity that enables the body of Christ to release the authority of God in the earth. Establishing God's purposes for a city or a nation requires a corporate authority, and according to David Demian, "This cannot be wielded by an individual or ministry or even a denomination, no matter how anointed they are or how much revelation they possess. To address spiritual entities controlling corporate spheres requires an authority from God that will only be released when there is a corporate body coming together in unity and in total submission to One Head."[24]

8. Wait for God's strategy and timing

When they knew they had a true word from the Lord that had been corporately discerned, they would go to God again until He would reveal to them His exact strategy—the steps God wanted them to take to fulfill the vision and the timing of those steps.

In September 1998, when the Watchmen team gathered together, one of the leaders shared that she had dreamed that the time had grown very late—eleven minutes to midnight—and she heard the Lord say, "It's the eleventh hour." All of them felt the dream was of the Lord, and the Lord impressed upon them to call a national repentance on November 11, 1998.[25]

Though it was short notice, more than six hundred people came to the meeting. David said that at one point "a wave of the presence of God swept across the room and people began dropping to their knees, overcome with travail and weeping...Suddenly I realized that we had landed in a kairos timing of God."[26]

David said, "I believe this kind of intimate knowledge and trust of the Lord must be our foundation if we want to be part of establishing the Kingdom of God on the earth today. As we move further down the timeline of human history into the 'end of days,' we won't just experience the occasional 'kairos moments' but entire kairos 'seasons' as God brings alignment and fulfillment to purposes that He has held in his heart for millennia."[27]

9. The remnant

In order to see God's kingdom established and our nation transformed, we don't have to amass a large number of people. Watchmen believe that they only need the critical mass, or the right number of the remnant that will please God's heart. If a remnant called by the Lord will posture itself in humility and brokenness and wait for His direction, He will extend the scepter of His authority to bring the government—and whoever else He wants—into conformity with the purpose of His will.

Throughout the Old Testament we see God using a remnant, a smaller group, to release victory for the whole. The number varies with each situation, from as few as one person (see Ezekiel 22:30, where God looked for someone to stand in the gap on behalf of the land) to the three hundred men God wanted to rout the enemy and win the victory for the whole nation.

10. Identification repentance and prophetic acts

David Demian and Gideon Chiu applied spiritual warfare weapons, including identification repentance and prophetic acts. Beginning with the First Nation in Canada, the Native American people and European people groups that emigrated to Canada, the French Quebec leaders marry their English counterpart in a marriage and burning of stakes to represent their total surrender and dedication to do God's will, gathering stones from all the various provinces of Canada to build a memorial altar to the Lord. In Malaysia, repentance and reconciliation took place between various native tribes, aborigines, and all other major cultural and racial groups. Repentance, the release of forgiveness, and reconciliation were done in Taiwan between the natives and Chinese immigrants. In Hong Kong, spiritual leaders from Japan and European nations that were part of the coalition of nations that fought and defeated China 170 years ago repented and asked for forgiveness before 16,000 participants, most of whom were from China.

11. Linking fathers and sons

Watchmen believe that a fatherless generation is an orphan generation, and the curse will come upon the land. However, the linking of the fathers and sons generations in covenant relationship results in generational blessings.

What are some of the measurable results?

After ten years' journey in Canada, David Demian mentioned six measurable results, which were also reported by Gideon Chiu of Vancouver, Canada:

1. During the banking and financial crisis that hit the United States and the world in 2008, Canadian banks remained strong.

2. Canada is the only nation among the G7 that has no debt.

3. Stephen Harper, the former prime minister of Canada, is a Christian.

4. The relationship between Canada and Israel was very strong during Harper's time.

5. A significant percentage of government party members of Parliament were Christians during Harper's time.

6. The Quebec Separatist Movement was soundly defeated in the national referendum and its leader lost in the election.

7. Before Stephen Harper stepped down, Canada had come from behind to be recognized as the most respected nation.

The nation of the Philippines: a model for a nation in the process of transformation

The Philippines was supposed to be the first Christian nation in Asia. After World War II, the Philippines was for a time regarded as the second wealthiest in East Asia, second only to Japan. In the 1960s its economic performance started being overtaken. The economy stagnated under the dictatorship of President Ferdinand Marcos as the regime spawned economic mismanagement and political volatility. The country suffered from slow economic growth and bouts of economic recession. Only in the 1990s with a program of economic liberalization did the economy begin to recover.[28]

Although the corruption, dictatorial regime, and poverty among its people left it looking like a failed state, with the overthrow of the Marcos regime through the People Power, the Philippines managed to progress through political reforms and economic liberalization.

> Poverty remains a critical issue in the Philippines where about 24 million people, more than 24 percent of the population, live below the poverty line even with economic growth averaging more than 5 percent a year since 2012. Successive governments have made limited progress in the fight on poverty, which stood at 22.6 percent in 2003, with corruption one of the biggest impediments to government action...
>
> [Benigno] Aquino, 54, won the presidency in 2010 after a campaign in which he pledged to fight corruption rampant among officials since dictator Ferdinand Marcos ruled the country from 1965 to 1986. Aquino's predecessor, Gloria Macapagal Arroyo, was arrested on charges of electoral fraud. Arroyo's predecessor Joseph Estrada, who is now Manila's mayor, was detained for six and a half years on corruption charges and later pardoned by Arroyo in 2007.
>
> **Economic Solution**
>
> Under Aquino, there has been some improvement with the country's score on the Transparency International Perceptions

corruption index, rising to 38 out of 100 in 2014 from 34 in 2012. Still, the country ranks 85 on the index of the 175 nations surveyed, where a No. 1 ranking signals the least corruption.

Sustaining economic growth may be the best way to improve conditions for the poor, and the Southeast Asian nation could end poverty within a generation if growth is sustained at 6 percent a year, World Bank economist Rogier van den Brink said on Jan. 14.[29]

According to Richard Javad Heydarian, in his 2014 article "The Philippines: The Next Asian Tiger economy?":

For the first time in its history, the Philippines managed to garner an "investment grade" status from the world's leading credit rating agencies in 2013. And most recently, the Standard & Poor's Ratings Services upgraded the country's credit rating to a notch above investment grade. In theory, this should allow the Philippines to attract greater foreign investment…

In recent years, the Philippines has emerged as one of the fastest growing economies in the world, impressively rivaling the dizzying growth rates of fellow Asian countries such as China.[30]

Following the strict control over the media during President Ferdinand Marcos's dictatorial regime, the press of the Philippines now allows its citizens to speak, debate, and read a wide range of information without fear of getting arrested, which has played a vital role in exposing corruption and injustice. I was amazed at their free media through newspapers, TV programs, and radio broadcasts that allow criticism of the ruling party and officials.

The question is, what happened in the spiritual sphere of the Philippines during the 1980s onward that enabled the nation to rise up again in strength and success? A convergence of political, spiritual, prayer, and transformational movements push the Philippines forward in her path for nation transformation.

1. PJM

The Philippines for Jesus Movement (PJM) is a coalition network of more than three hundred churches that started in the 1980s. Founding president,

Brother Eddie Villanueva; secretary-general, Deputy Governor Diwa Guinigundo; and Magtanggol Guinigundo together played an important role in the spiritual life of the Philippines. In the coalition's early days, the idea came to one day in the future see God placed on the pesos, the Philippine currency. This massive church movement played a vital role in the transformation of the nation, beginning with the rededication of the Philippines to the Lord Jesus Christ during a massive rally in the 1980s, during Corazon (Cory) Aquino's presidency. Brother Eddie Villanueva has the habit of making the prophetic declaration, "Jesus is Lord over the Philippines," in every meeting he preaches. PJM has a regular weekly TV program called *PJM Forum* and another, *God and Nation*, to discuss political and spiritual issues affecting the nation.

2. Intercessors for the Philippines

Bishop Dan Balais, the president of Intercessors for the Philippines, managed to raise more than 100,000 intercessors for the nation of the Philippines. He worked closely with Brother Eddie Villanueva and Bishop Leo Alconga and was later involved in PJM. This prayer movement undergirds the nation through various political crises, disasters, and challenges facing the nation. By interfacing with PJM and working closely with Brother Eddie Villanueva, this movement was able to penetrate the whole nation both in the cities and villages.

In 2013 Bishop Dan was successful in bringing together the top leadership of PJM, the Pentecostal/Charismatic network of churches, and PCEC, the Philippines Council of Evangelical Churches. For the first time leaders from these two major evangelical groups were united through a series of meetings and a retreat. This resulted in the two groups joining hands for the success of organizing the Asia for Christ Congress in September 2013 in Manila. President Benigno S. Aquino III graced the congress with his presence and gave a short address. I was present as vice-president of the Asia for Christ Movement, and Brother Eddie Villanueva led in prayer for the president and the Philippines. With such unity in the body of Christ in the Philippines, as the spiritual fathers walk together in love and covenant relationship and pray, the nation will be transformed.

3. Touching Heaven, Changing Earth

The Touching Heaven, Changing Earth Movement was launched on

September 15, 2005, at the Philippine International Convention Center in Manila with the BSP (Bangko Sentral ng Pilipinas, or Philippines Central Bank) under the leadership of Deputy Governor Diwa Guinigundo acting as advisor. A second conference at the BSP Assembly Hall was held in 2006, and since then hundreds of churches represented by hundreds of pastors, elders, and church leaders were reached in a series of provincial conferences. I was involved as one of the speakers for these two conferences. From then onward, the Touching Heaven, Changing Earth movement has reached thirty-seven cities in a series of regional conferences. This includes conferences in San Fernando, La Union; Davao City; Cebu City; Tagbilaran, Bohol; Dumaguete, Negros Oriental; Urdaneta, Pangasinan; Legazpi, Albay; Naga, Camarines Sur; Cabanatuan, Nueva Ecija; San Jose, Nueva Ecija; Batangas City; Olongapo City; Puerto Princesa, Palawan; and Dipolog City.

A brochure produced by Brother Cezar F. Arceo (czarceo@yahoo.com) describes its vision. The Touching Heaven, Changing Earth movement envisions the Philippines worshipping Jesus as a nation. It aims to expand the kingdom of God, take the forces of darkness out of the marketplace, and to help transform the Philippines by impressing the importance of touching the heart of God. The thrust of this movement is to unite the body of Christ and help redeem the Philippines from the oppressive spirit of poverty and disunity. This national movement had coordinated conferences with Philippines for Jesus Movement (PJM), the Intercessors for the Philippines, Philippines Council of Evangelical Churches (PCEC), and other national and local pastoral movements. Their vision for the future of the Philippines—that is, for their nation's children, and children's children—can be expressed as:

+ High growth, high employment, high income
+ Public infrastructure, services excellent
+ Respect for law and authority
+ Illegal occupancy unnecessary, a thing of the past
+ High moral standard in public service
+ Strong air, sea, and land defenses
+ Overseas employment limited to missionaries
+ A respected member of the league of nations

They plan to have Island Congresses with the agenda for church unity and nation transformation soon to be followed by national congress. This is to launch the Philippines church as a social force for nation transformation: good and responsible governance, values formation, economic revolution, educational competitiveness, and cultural renaissance.

One vital component that is coming to convergence with other factors mentioned earlier, including spiritual warfare principles, apostles, and prophets working with intercessors, is the marketplace. Here in the Philippines model, marketplace apostles and prophets like Deputy Governor Diwa Guinigundo and Brother Cezar Arceo are calling both the nuclear church and the church in the marketplace to rise up and contribute to the transformation of their nation.

While the nuclear church, with their apostles, prophets, pastors, teachers, evangelists, and intercessors, is engaged in various spiritual issues like intercession and spiritual warfare, the marketplace people are to rise into their rightful places in various cultural domains, including the government, business, education, media, arts and entertainment. This will result in reformational laws being passed in Congress, good governance, economic growth, and at the same time seeing poverty and corruption being eradicated in a major way. Numerous bills aimed at eradicating corruption have been passed in Congress over the past ten years, various schemes to eliminate poverty were passed, and projects that benefited the poor were also carried out. On June 17, 2013, *USA TODAY* ran a special edition under the theme, "Rise and Shine with the Philippines," on the occasion when President Obama visited the Philippines. The writer claimed that one of the government's most successful schemes to date is Pantawid Pamilya, or Family Subsistence, piloted in 2007:

> Currently, 3 million poor households receive small monthly grants for keeping their children healthy and enrolled in school...[President Aquino claimed] "These past two years, we have also breathed new life into the idea that government is there to work for its people. We have focused on fulfilling our mandate to uplift the common Filipino by spending significant portions of our budget on social services—most prominently our Pantawid Pamilya Program, which is helping 3 million households from sinking further into poverty, and is giving them the resources to lift themselves out of their situations. We are giving their children the chance at proper education. We are requiring them

to see medical professionals for regular check-ups. In short, government is finally giving our people what they rightfully deserve."[31]

In Dipolog City, while the Touching Heaven, Changing Earth Movement conference was being conducted in early September 2014, Credit Surety Fund (CSF) was launched by the BSP led by Deputy Governor Diwa Guinigundo the following day, followed by a signing ceremony. Credit Surety Fund is empowering MSME (Micro, Small, Medium Enterprises) by giving them access to bank credits even though they may not have collateral or good credit records. The CSF pools contributions from well-managed and well-capitalized cooperatives/NGOs, partners with government financial institutions like the Land Bank, the DBP, and the Industrial Guarantee Loan Fund, as well as the local government units including both city and provincial governments, and use such pooled funds as surety against loans of cooperatives. "The Fund is deposited in a trustee bank and invested in high-yielding government securities."[32]

Diwa remarked, "In the last six years, the CSF has evolved far beyond just being one of the BSP's key initiatives for inclusive growth. It has become an important social covenant that resolves to put a closure to economic powerlessness among many small entrepreneurs. Indeed in the past, MSMEs were virtually denied of many opportunities to progress because they cannot borrow from banks simply because they have nothing to offer as collateral. This has been a sad commentary on the non-inclusiveness of our banking system. High cost of borrowings from informal sources of credit and the lack of available working capital for business expansion weaken the growth of MSMEs and consequently slacken their contribution to economic growth. Through the CSF, MSMEs can borrow a multiple contribution of P 100 thousand."[33]

In the book *Why Nations Fail: The Origins of Power, Prosperity, and Poverty*, the authors stated, "Countries need inclusive economic and political institutions to break out of the cycle of poverty."[34] According to the authors, "We will refer to political institutions that are sufficiently centralized and pluralistic as inclusive political institutions. When either of these conditions fails, we will refer to the institutions as extractive political institutions."[35]

The Philippines definitely has been moving toward inclusive economic and political institutions. I have no doubt the country is breaking out of the cycle of poverty, no longer a failed nation.

CONCLUSION
WHERE DO WE GO FROM HERE?

$\mathcal{S}$EVERAL CHALLENGES ARE facing the church in the future with regard to the transformation of nations. The first is the goal of transforming one's own community, city, or nation. The second is the measurement of transformation (How do you know transformation is taking place, or has taken place?) Third, we must identify models of communities, cities, or nations that are in the process of transformation. Fourth, how do we sustain the victory of seeing transformation taking place? Fifth, how can the church as an agency of the kingdom of God further expand His kingdom?

The church must determine its role in this world. There are four types of models I can think of, using the analogy of boats and ships. The first model is the fishing boat. Many small local churches are operating like fishing vessels, mostly small, and some large ones are like trawlers. Their main concern is fishing—that is, winning souls for the Lord and taking care of the needs of their families. Some are more successful than others.

The second model is the cruise ship. Currently this seems to be the ultimate model for its effectiveness in drawing high numbers of people. Yes, it is entertaining; catering to all types of needs and has multiple ministries. The people seem to have an enjoyable time like a cruise ship. Megachurches, while adopting the cruise ship model can be very powerful when they know their destiny and are willing to fulfill God's purpose for their communities, cities and nations. Hence, cruise ships can be turned into aircraft carriers.

The third model is the refugee ship. This is the result of the pessimistic teaching of eschatological escapism; that is, as the world is in the last days, the anti-Christ will be revealed and the world only goes from bad to worse. Christ is coming soon, and so the church is awaiting rapture from this evil world. Therefore, the entire idea is to abandon the earth because it cannot be saved. Thus the church model is the refugee ship, and this model frequently rejects the positive view of the earth in future such as "the kingdoms of this world have become the kingdoms of our Lord and of His Christ, and He shall reign forever and ever!" (Rev. 11:15).

The fourth model is the battleship. God has called the church to war in the spiritual sense. The kingdom of God is expanded by conquering the seven areas of influence in nations and cultures. According to David Cannistraci, the word "apostles" comes from the root word *apostolos*, meaning one who is sent forth or sent away from one place to another to accomplish a specific mission. An apostle is an emissary or ambassador, and the term also refers to the "admiral who commanded the fleet or to the colony that was founded by the admiral."[1] Therefore, apostles are to establish God's kingdom in other ethnic groups by planting churches, or in various spheres of society in the case of marketplace or workplace apostles.

THE GOAL OF TRANSFORMING A NATION

From what I have gathered over the years, transformation for a nation varies from "fulfilling God's purpose" to becoming "a Christian nation." Some have suggested that in a "Christian nation," more than 50 percent of the population should be Christians. However, I have not discovered a consistently agreed-upon goal. Yet in Psalm 33:12 we read, "Blessed is the nation whose God is the LORD, the people He has chosen as His own inheritance." This verse seems to suggest that the people and leaders of this nation dedicate their lives and their nation to God.

THE MEASUREMENTS FOR A NATION THAT HAS BEEN TRANSFORMED

It is interesting to note that Mark W. Pfeifer, writing in his book *Alignment*, says that we need a new definition of success in the church.[2] Taking the New Testament's emphasis on cities, also known as territories, into account, he suggests that instead of using church attendance and membership to define success, the definition of a successful church is "the condition of your territory." He reasoned that if "the condition of your territory" was the commonly accepted definition of success among pastors in a given area, things would begin to change. "People would be equipped for ministry in the church and in the workplace. Each pastor would sense his or her responsibility to do whatever it takes to transform the community."[3] Then he suggested using the template of subduing and dominating the seven cultural mountains as an excellent way to change territories. That to me is a new idea to measure the success of a local church.

Some measurements being used include the rate of poverty, crimes, unemployment, economic growth, conversions, having a Christian prime minister, churches being multiplied, getting rid of corrupt government, a rise in the standard of living, and good government. Some suggest using Gross Domestic Product (GDP) growth, while others argue for the Quality of Life Index developed by the Economist Intelligence Unit (EIU) in 2005 as better measurement.[4] Japan and Singapore are good examples of developed nations with little or no poverty, but I don't believe they can be considered nations that are "transformed" because they cannot be put in the same category as "whose God is the Lord." Yet they fulfilled most of the measurements mentioned. Surely this issue will be debated more in the future.

MODELS OF TRANSFORMED COMMUNITIES, CITIES, AND NATIONS

I am sure more models of transformation of cities, communities, and nations are forthcoming. George Otis Jr. produced some documentary films on the topic and has made them available in DVD format. With many more exponents of nation transformation, and with many lessons learned from some case studies, God will challenge individuals and churches to be agencies for change. We must expect new ideas and study new ways that God has worked in various parts of the world that ultimately resulted in the transformation of nations and societies.

HOW DO WE SUSTAIN THE VICTORY AFTER BEING TRANSFORMED?

History records that the United States of America is a nation that was developed on Judeo-Christian principles. Over the years it has undergone many changes and become a secular state. The same goes for Australia. When the United States won the wars in Iraq and Afghanistan, they allowed the enemy to return and regain ground, as they did not have clear blueprints for nation building in nations that do not have Judeo-Christian principles.

How Can the Church as an Agency of the Kingdom of God Further Expand His Kingdom?

The last decade, the mission call for the church was to evangelize and plant churches among more than 4,500 unreached people groups by the AD2000 and Beyond Movement. Now is the time for the church to replace that mission call with the mandate for nation transformation. For this to happen, the church will have to change its methods for training and equipping people. The vision of the church has to be realigned to the call to see communities, cities, and nations transformed. We may have to rethink, retrain, and restrategize the church and mission agencies for this greater mandate. Jun Vencer, prominent Christian leader and statesman from the Philippines, former World Evangelical Fellowship International Director, in his address at the Asia for Christ Congress held at PICC in Manila on November 14, 2012, warned delegates that economic indicators alone are not sufficient to measure the transformation of nations.

APPENDIX 1
NATIONS

Written and Reported by Dr. Dexter Low

Prophetic Proclamation by Pedro Ferdinand de Quiros, Day of Pentecost, 14th May, 1606

Let the heavens, the earth, the waters with all their creatures, and those present, witness that I, Captain Pedro Ferdinand de Quiros...in the name of Jesus Christ...hoist this emblem of the holy cross on which His person was crucified and whereon He gave His life for the ransom and remedy of all the human race...on this day of Pentecost, 14th May...I take possession of all this part of the south as far as the pole in the name of Jesus...which from now on shall be called the southern land of the Holy Ghost...and this always and forever...and to the end that to all natives, in all the said lands, the holy and sacred evangel may be preached zealously and openly.[1]

What I expect to be accomplished in our meetings in Melbourne, Australia

A woman intercessor received an impression of a sailing ship at sea during a River of Life core intercessors team prayer meeting in February 2015, then sensed a word from the Lord: "There is a north wind coming; we who are on the ship are to be prepared for this unfurling our sails."

I believe that "Wind" of the great move of God is what Australia needs to rid itself of the orphan spirit in the nation. It is to bring fathers together and release the heart of the father to the nations, linking with the sons, walking together and hearing the voice of God corporately in full consecration of hearts, resulting in a great move of the Spirit. Australia's destiny is linked with Asia, and it is time for the Australian fathers to catch the north wind in their sails. In times past Australia has contributed much in missions to all of Asia as tens of thousands of missionaries were sent all over the world. Now this team from the north is coming to Australia at its own expense to bless Australia, to share with Australian fathers what God is doing and humbly request them to align their nation with Asia in this great move of the Spirit.

Our role as a team from the north, including China, Canada, Hong Kong, and Malaysia, is like that of mere midwives to assist in the birth of the Family Journey of Australia. We believe that the vision will be birthed at the meetings and that the Australian fathers will carry the mandate and vision forward.

Fathers from the marketplace representing all the domains will be welcome, as their role is significant. The transformation of the nation can only take place when the Kingdom of God comes to all the various spheres of influence, when strategic God- and kingdom-centered people are placed there to initiate reforms.

A convergence of marketplace people in various domains, with the Prayer Movement of Fathers linking hearts and aligning to God's kingdom purposes for the nation, will result not only in revival in the church but transformation of the society and nation. This is vital to see Australia fulfill her destiny as a nation that will release men and women to advance the kingdom of God in the nations of the world. Australia has vast potential to do that, having not only capable and mature men and women of God but also strength in finance, know-how, business models, modern technologies, and training.

The infrastructure has been set and is being built rapidly. In Melbourne, Peter Kentley gathered strategic men and women of Australia to take all the domains for the kingdom of God. In Adelaide, Mark Mudri initiated the KFC, Kingdom Facilitation Center, to function in a similar way. What is needed is the "Wind of God from the North" to blow into the sails.

I believe the meetings both in Adelaide and Melbourne will awaken a move of God where fathers will link their hearts to the next generation of sons and rise to walk together hand in hand. Similarly, I would love to see Australian fathers link up with fathers from the North—China, Japan, South Korea, Hong Kong, Macau, Taiwan, and Malaysia.

I have seen this building up personally as I took part in three recent gatherings.

Hong Kong, April, Pre-Asian Gathering in preparation for a large gathering in July

The Lord knitted our hearts together during our meetings and worship, and I was deeply touched that these fathers from China, South Korea, and Japan accepted me to be part of their circle.

Kuching, Sarawak, Malaysia

Fathers from various tribes of Sarawak and Sabah linked their hearts with Orang Asli (Aborigines from West Malaysia) and Chinese. Because the natives are the "First Born" and are "Guardians" of the land, they had authority when they consecrated themselves to the Lord and then the land of Malaysia to Him. We sense that a major shift is taking place in the spiritual sphere that will result in major ramifications in Malaysia and felt that it was no wonder when a rainbow appeared after the gatherings.

Kobe, Japan

The gathering in Japan was truly historic, coming seventy years after the end of World War I. Japan has the redemptive gift of being a "warring nation" but used it wrongly to conquer, causing much hardship and cruelty. For seventy years Japan lost her warring spirit and the church remained small (less than 1 percent nationwide) until now. It is time for Japan to arise and take her place, linking hearts with China and South Korea.

South Korea shares with the global body of Christ the gift of prayer. China, after seventy years of persecution and the imprisonment of many of their fathers, has emerged strong, with the redemptive gift of an "overcoming nation," as they loved not their lives unto death. One of the fathers who shared on the first night had just been released from prison. For the first time, he had a passport and was able to travel to Japan. Many of the fathers of the underground churches have been imprisoned many times. From 1 million in 1949 when the Communists took over, where they were supposed to be destroyed, there are today at least 100 million believers.[2] In the 2012 Asia Homecoming Gathering in Hong Kong, 16,000 people came, 80 percent of which were from mainland China. Three "sons" representing China, South Korea, and Japan linked their hands together and made a covenant to love each other and not to be influenced by the past, the media, or others, to look ahead into the future and to bless other nations.

Japan was partners with Germany in World War II seventy years ago. The Germans, wanting to conquer Europe and Japan and also wanting to conquer Asia, came together to make a covenant of war. In Kobe, they repented from their evil and gave themselves as partners for peace to the nations.

Let us expect the birth of a great move in Australia through our meetings both in Adelaide and Melbourne. Can Australia have a similar move? The answer is, "Yes, when we are willing to make time and come together," for the same Spirit that works great things in the north is willing to come south. Open your sails—i.e., your hearts—to receive the "Wind from the North."

Gideon Chiu, Vancouver

Pastor Gideon Chiu in Vancouver has been the spiritual father and adoptive brother of David Demian, the Egyptian doctor and founder of Watchmen for the Nations. With the spiritual leadership of Dr. John White, Bob Birch, and Jim Watt, Pastor Gideon's ten years of Family Journey has seen Canada turn around in a remarkable way. Presently, they are making a great impact in China, uniting five streams of underground churches, one of which involves 50,000 churches, and another 60,000, together totalling about 35 million believers. Taiwan especially is being greatly impacted as the natives unite with Chinese churches in covenant relationships, walking and praying together for the betterment of the nation. Family Journey has also touched Hong Kong, Macau, Malaysia, Japan, and South Korea.

Pastor Gideon Chiu is a father with a father's heart. He is a connector and catalyst, bringing fathers and sons of the nation together to see the destiny of nations fulfilled and His kingdom come. A Chinese Canadian, he speaks both Chinese and English and studied at the Fuller Theological Seminary and Regent College in Canada. He, his wife, May, and their several children reside in Vancouver.

China

The strategic "son" of the Chinese churches has been in the marketplace for twelve years and pastors a number of home churches. He stands as a witness to share about many things God is doing in China, and often serves as a facilitator under his spiritual father. He is skilled in administration, information technology, and organization. He speaks and writes in Chinese and English, and is married with one son.

Andrew Ho, Hong Kong

A father from Hong Kong, Andrew Ho is the prime mover and organizer for most citywide events in his area, including various crusades and outreach efforts with Reinhard Bonnke, Hillsong Music, and the like. He is a marketplace publisher and distributor of Christian books, an earnest supporter of many projects and movements with a heart's cry to see results. He testifies concerning Family Journey, where fathers in the nation join their hearts with sons and walk together over many years. They are making a difference in China, Hong Kong, Macau, Japan, and South Korea. He speaks both Chinese and English.

APPENDIX 2
TAKING *the* KINGDOM *of* GOD
into the MARKETPLACE

*A Vision of Transforming Cities and Nations through the
Marketplace Saints and Their Occupations
Written and Reported by Peter Kentley, River of Life Conference,
Melbourne, Australia, Global Marketplace Exchange*

*A*CONVERSION OF PRAYER movements, apostolic network, and marketplace movement.

INTRODUCTION

Christian Federation (CF) is a coalition of Kingdom Partners (KP) dedicated to glorifying Jesus in every domain of our city and nation (John 17:18–23, Col. 1:15–20).

Kingdom Partners are nodes or intersections in the net of the kingdom of God spread across church and marketplace domains. We work by relationship and referral instead of independence and competition. Every kingdom partner is committed to the success of every other partner under God.

CF builds relationships that collaborate in the exchange of ideas, referrals, connectivity, experience, resources, and mutual support, and is a pioneering contributor to church and marketplace re-formation to bless our nation under God (Gen. 1:28, Ps. 33:12).

We see the future body of Christ working in united formation to bring glory to Jesus in every domain of the nation. To this end, we are working together to develop a connecting hub that accelerates church and marketplace re-formation by Word and Spirit.

Re-formation is about recognition that Jesus is just as much King of the marketplace as He is High Priest of the church. On this basis we encourage church and marketplace leaders to connect in collaborative relationships that accelerate the application of the Lord's Prayer, Jesus's John 17 prayer, the Great Commandment, and the Great Commission into the marketplaces of the nation. This is implemented through the everyday occupations of the saints. We lead with the prayer of Psalm 32:8, the process of Proverbs 3:5–6, and the promise of Psalm 33:12.

The Mandate of the Word of God in Genesis 1:28, Psalm 110, Daniel 2:31–45, Acts 2:34, Romans 9:30–33, 1 Corinthians 15:24, Ephesians 1:22, Colossians 1:15–20, Hebrews 2:8, 1 Peter 2:4–9, Revelation 11:15 and 19:11–16, is for the body of Christ to bring forth the divine order and blessing of the kingdom of God in an otherwise disorderly world.

As portrayed in Psalm 110, the Scriptures are clear that the enemies of Jesus will become a footstool for His feet. Jesus will rule in the midst of His enemies, and His troops will be willing in the day of His battle. This leads to the great hope of the psalmist:

> But the plans of the LORD stand firm forever, the purposes of his heart through all generations. Blessed is the nation whose God is the LORD.
>
> —PSALM 33:11–12, NIV

The term *domains* can be read synonymously with parallel terms such as *gates, cultural mountains, sectors* or *spheres of influence.* Where a domain of society honors the supremacy of Christ, it becomes a King's Domain or king*dom* where "Your kingdom come. Your will be done on earth as it is in heaven" (Matt. 6:10, Col. 1:15–20). Similarly the terms *state* and *marketplace* should be used interchangeably in this context.

REVIVAL OR RE-FORMATION?

History tells us that revivals are relatively short lived and often leave communities in worse shape than before they began (Matt. 12:43–45). Unless there is re-formation where the culture is *cleaned up and occupied* by kingdom people (Gen. 1:28) the culture of the marketplace reverts to disorder and overwhelms the church.

Church and state re-formation

By this we do not mean a continuation of the reformation started by Martin Luther's 95 Theses in 1517. That protest was largely over with the 1999 *Lutheran World Federation and Catholic Church's joint declaration on the doctrine of justification.*

The *re-formation* we are seeking comes out of the reality that the Western church is losing the battle with culture over the preeminence of Christ in our cities and nations (Col. 1:15–20). When an army is losing a battle, it needs to withdraw and re-form by rearming, bringing in fresh troops, and restrategizing how to win the war. And win we will, because it is written (see Daniel 7:21–22; Revelation 13:7 and 17:12–14). *This battle plan of re-formation drives our conference.*

But *re-form to what?* The answer to this critical question is found in rediscovery of what Jesus meant in the establishment of His *ecclesia* in Matthew 16:13–20.

The ecclesia of Jesus:

1. *hears and understands* the Great Command, the Great Commission, the Lord's Prayer, and Jesus's prayer of John 17;

2. commits *to live* according to these principles; and

3. commits *to work together* to provide everyday leadership based on these principles of the kingdom so as to produce good fruit that lasts (Matt. 13:23, John 15:16).

CHURCH AND MARKETPLACE CONFERENCE

An annual conference has been established to bring together leaders from church and the marketplace to work together in long-term strategy to bring the influence of the kingdom into the domains / gates / spheres / cultural mountains of the nation.

Domain illustration[1]
Twenty-year vision

The discovery of each domain organization's purpose is in the context of a twenty-year vision, where we believe that Christ has returned in the context of Psalm 110. What would each domain look like as a King's domain rather than in a secular context?

> The LORD says to my lord: "Sit at my right hand until I make your enemies a footstool for your feet."
> The LORD will extend your mighty scepter from Zion, saying, "Rule in the midst of your enemies!" Your troops will be willing on

your day of battle. Arrayed in holy splendor, your young men will come to you like dew from the morning's womb.

The LORD has sworn and will not change his mind: "You are a priest forever, in the order of Melchizedek."

The Lord is at your right hand; he will crush kings on the day of his wrath. He will judge the nations, heaping up the dead and crushing the rulers of the whole earth. He will drink from a brook along the way, and so he will lift his head high.

—PSALM 110, NIV

Current-year objectives
What are two current-year *domain objectives* that your organization is working toward in the context of your twenty-year vision?

Convergence objectives
What are our two highest-priority *national objectives* that can only be achieved if three or more domains work in collaboration?

Domain cultural influence
What is the peak body to which your group must become a respected contributor if it is to bring kingdom influence to your domain?

Who, when, where
Each domain nominates a team of three leaders who will represent their domain at the annual conference. These leaders make a plan to determine who, when, and where they will meet to catalyse and pursue with clarity and perseverance their domain objectives, convergence objectives, and progress reports and proposals for the next annual conference.

Who we are
We are a coalition of Kingdom Partners comprising individuals, local churches, Christian organizations, and marketplace microchurches (Matt. 18:20) who are of the same heart and mind *to glorify Jesus in every domain of our city and nation*. By means of "netweaving," different nodes of the net are joined together to function according to the will and ways of God.

AUTHOR'S NOTE

*I*N THIS BOOK my goal has been to inspire the church globally to focus on city and region transformation. To some this may seem to be an overwhelming mission, but if the fivefold ministers come together in agreement, good testimonies will begin to come forth. As you study the stories in the Bible, the testimonies will become more than just stories; they become blueprints for transformation. The Great Commission is a mandate to disciple nations—but how should this be accomplished?

> Then Jesus came to them and said, "All authority in heaven and on earth has been given to me. Therefore go and make disciples of all nations, baptizing them in the name of the Father and of the Son and of the Holy Spirit, and teaching them to obey everything I have commanded you. And surely I am with you always, to the very end of the age."
> —MATTHEW 28:18–20, NIV

I challenge you to seek the Lord for the blueprint for your city or region. What is the Lord revealing to the leaders in your area? The following is an overview of city transformation in the city of Adelaide in South Australia. This will provide some practical points for your consideration.

I have included two current models of transformation: the city of Adelaide and the nation of Sri Lanka.

REPORT *to the* INTERNATIONAL COALITION *of* APOSTLES

From Adelaide, South Australia, October 2013
Written and Reported by Mark Mudri

November 2011—The prophetic mandate

In November 2011, leaders from many nations gathered in Melaka, Malaysia, to celebrate the 500th or the 10th jubilee of the gospel entering Asia. In 1511 the wealth and the Judeo-Christian worldview had sailed into the straits of Melaka under the flag of Saint George and the East India trading company.

After the celebration Apostle Naomi Dowdy, based in Singapore, gave a prophetic mandate:

+ Go and break the curse of poverty over your city.
+ Keep gathering leadership and building unity, and not only pray but reason together.

Christmas 2011—Emerging leaders in unity

A few days before Christmas, leaders gathered at an international hotel for a meal and to reason together. Leaders included pastors, political activists, inventors, IT experts, a trainer of F18 fighter pilots, lawyers, the federal head of a Christian political party, head of Teen Challenge, the head of the Singapore Australia Business Council, and various other leaders. On that occasion it was important to specifically call the men of the city to a high place. One of the outcomes was that the general of the armed forces was invited to speak at the city prayer breakfast, attracting a historic 1,200 people. Another outcome was that one of our key leaders facilitated, with the general's endorsement, the release of "Faith Under Fire" training series, which explains the Judeo-Christian foundation of our nation, to the entire armed forces.

We began to witness the commanded blessing whenever leaders who celebrate other leaders would gather together.

March 2012—Visit by Apostles John P. Kelly and Chris Peterson to the heart of the city

In about February of 2012, we learned that Apostles John P. Kelly and Chris Peterson would be visiting Adelaide. At fairly short notice, 133 leaders registered for a function in the town hall.

We were delighted that the Lord Mayor opened the meeting, and teaching emerged about the importance of opening the civil and the ecclesiastical gates of a city. Apostles Kelly and Peterson worked beautifully in tandem to teach about covenant and the true gospel of the kingdom. Leaders came from as far away as Malaysia, Singapore, India, and throughout Australia. The meeting culminated in Communion and was a massive demonstration of unity to principalities and powers over the city.

The very same evening, we had a second function at the Crystal Room overlooking Parliament House. Apostle Kelly stirred the audience, and there was significant ministry to senior leaders following the meeting.

The following morning, a further group of senior leaders met at one of the most significant churches in the city. Apostle Kelly accurately prophesied about planting churches in Singapore and New York. The leadership of the church was stunned as this was quietly being contemplated for some time.

It is clear that since the visit of Apostle Kelly and Chris Peterson, the momentum has greatly accelerated in Adelaide for the advancement of the kingdom.

January 2012—Establishment of KFC (Kingdom Facilitation Centre)

In response to the pending visit of Apostle Kelly, the KFC was formed as a small but incredibly diverse and talented standing army.

The Kingdom Facilitation Centre solely exists to facilitate and support leaders and emerging leaders in the seven mountains that shape culture. It is an oasis and a gathering of leaders across the denominations and vocations that are determined to see the fulfillment of the prayer of Jesus in John 17, that we would truly be one.

Leaders gather for prayer every Thursday and for strategic implementation every Monday. The meetings have been undergirded by prophetic worship by Margot and more than thirty years of prophetic and pastoral experience by Joan.

A reoccurring pattern has been observed whereby leaders significant in their fields are attacked relationally, emotionally, and financially.

The KFC was established to refresh, equip, and introduce leaders around specific citywide projects.

August 2012—Visit by Peter Tsukahira

We hosted Peter Tsukahira, author of *My Father's Business*. This was a joint collaboration between Full Gospel Businessmen's Fellowship International (FGBMFI), the International Christian Chamber of Commerce, Youth With A Mission, and the Australian House of Prayer for All Nations. Peter taught us how God is transforming the marketplace and that the seven mountains mandate was given in a form to Moses encompassing all the ingredients necessary to transform society.

BUSINESS

October 27, 2012—FGBMFI moves to the seven mountains mandate

We were joined by senior gatekeepers from Singapore to teach and assist the national organization with implementing the seven mountains mandate and overcoming the spirit of fear and intimidation.

> We saw the Nephilim there (the descendants of Anak come from the Nephilim). We seemed like grasshoppers in our own eyes, and we looked the same to them.
>
> —NUMBERS 13:33, NIV

The son of the former health minister of Malaysia was hosted in Adelaide. Several ministries along with the KFC assisted in hosting this key marketplace champion.

July 26, 2013—Visit by Apostle Tan Tek Seng

Apostle Tan Tek Seng, former national president of the Full Gospel Businessmen's Fellowship Malaysia, challenged a full house, and again a number of ministries worked together to support the dinner.

The publisher printed testimonies in a secular book, *BBQ to Boardroom: Inspirational Stories of Successful South Australian Men in Business*, which graces hundreds of reception rooms across the city. Through the book we have been able to pray for, evangelize, and discover highly ethical pre-Christians.

GOVERNMENT

July 12, 2003—Visit by Ugandan High Court Judge

The KFC assisted with the Peace In Our Time conference, which was attended by a former High Court Judge from Uganda. The Judge has since been named the Director of Public Prosecutions in Uganda, overseeing 500 lawyers and prosecutors to further justice and righteousness in the legal system. While the Judge was in Adelaide, we held a special city leaders' prayer meeting where leaders from business, commerce, politics, and churches; a former premier; and a mayor gathered together in the highest boardroom in the heart of the city. We got on our knees and repented and had Communion together.

The Judge also met with our Director of Public Prosecutions, and an exchange of information began which could see the establishment of victims of crime impact statements being adopted in Uganda. We also spoke of the beginnings of a bilateral child adoption treaty between Uganda and South Australia to abolish the current practice where it can take five years and $50,000 for one child to be adopted. A meeting with the archbishop also advanced support for the fledgling legal system in South Sudan.

Law Reforms—Australia

The approach of identifying and supporting champions in their fields has borne fruit in the form of the first change to our criminal appeal system in one hundred years.

A new law has been passed in this state creating a new right of appeal which is now being considered by all of the states and territories in Australia. The pioneer in that field is becoming a world authority on miscarriages of justice. One of the strategies was to fill the Parliament and Senate committee rooms when the issue was being investigated. Our champion had proven that we had been in breach of the International Covenant on Human Rights for over thirty years. The abomination of the innocent being punished and the guilty walking free was now challenged.

We have been working with governmental leaders and providing them with state-of-the-art practice on issues such as human trafficking, and assisting with building bridges with refugees and migrant communities. Christian lawyers have also resisted the push toward same-sex marriage and have given evidence at the Parliamentary committee level. An international submission has been made to the Inter-American Court of Human Rights in relation to this issue by lawyers from Canada, England, and Australia.

World Prayer Assembly—Jakarta, Indonesia

We were privileged to be invited as speakers for the government track and took part in a worship service with 110,000 people in a sports stadium. The Indonesian Christian Lawyers Fellowship was also birthed as a result of encouraging one key Indonesian lawyer.

ARTS AND ENTERTAINMENT

Suing the Devil

Suing the Devil is the first Christian film produced in Australia in one hundred years. The film features the well-known Malcolm McDowell (who shot Captain Kirk in *Star Trek*). The KFC team gathered around its Adelaide-based producer, and six theatres were booked and sold out. Upon its DVD release in America, *Suing the Devil* climbed to number 12 on the Walmart On Demand charts within a few weeks, outselling *Johnny English* and *The Muppets*.[1]

Party for the Lord

One of the visions brought to the KFC by a dear prophetic leader was that the Lord wanted a party at the heart of the arts district of Adelaide. One of the world's greatest harp players and classical guitarists, Alvaro Sanchez, and a Grammy award nominee and worship leader from Saddleback church, Dr. Enoch, flew from America as part of a demonstration of everything that is beautiful, noble, and pure about the arts. The vision included prophetic writing, art, dance, jewelry, photography, food, and African choirs. It was a celebration of the beauty and majesty of the creative genius of the Lord.

INVENTIONS AND PROJECTS

We have been amazed at the extraordinary projects that we have been entrusted with facilitating in some way. A partial list includes the following:

+ affordable housing called iHomes;

- supplement to a cancer fighting regimen that restores the health of the woman;

- natural perfumery;

- a Christian clothing label called "Eternal Ride Apparel";

- resin made from waste and refuse that sets harder than concrete;

- revolutionary personal transport called "Chariot Skates"; and

- a methodology that could revolutionize the way business is valued.

The KFC is assisting in a small way the process from embracing an embryonic idea to commercialization. An ultimate goal is a covenant bank with a standing army of well-resourced experts entrusted to implement the pending great transfer of wealth.

FAMILY

Redefining pro-life

The shedding of innocent blood and the heartbreak of innocent women suffering from post-abortion grief is an issue which must be courageously and sensitively engaged. Last week we again rented the town hall, and while we confronted the culture of death, we proclaimed and celebrated the Author of Life. An African choir, testimonies from an owner of a cafe next to the abortion mill, a blind leader of the 40 Days for Life prayer campaign, a testimony of a precious woman from Operation Outcry, and an international healing ministry assembled together to bring this issue to the light and promote healing and restoration to those who are hurting.

April 2013—Advocates International

We led a twenty-four—strong delegation of legal professionals and students to Hong Kong in a joint summit between the University of Hong Kong, Faith and Law across the Globe, Campus Crusade for Christ, and Advocates International. We met as the Global Council of Advocates International and prayed to implement the strategies relating to human trafficking and other key issues affecting the regions. Attendees included many legal champions, from law students to a former Supreme Court Judge, the head of the Justice

Unit for the Salvation Army, a former commander of the Special Air Service (SAS), and key lawyers.

Advocates International represents 30,000 lawyers in 150 nations. It is the writer's dream to see greater cooperation between these reformers and revolutionaries and the apostolic prophetic movement across the globe.

The lawyers have demonstrated an unexpected and inspiring level of unity. If such unity is possible amongst lawyers it is possible with any group on Earth.

April 2012—Bridge between East and West

As often as possible, we strengthen the bridge between Asia and Australia. Apostles Naomi Dowdy and Chris Peterson hosted a meeting of leaders from the nations. A significant delegation from KFC attended the key strategic regional meetings.

Apostle Dexter Low and Lily, his delightful wife, from Malaysia, have ministered to leaders at the weekly city leader's prayer meeting in May 2013 and have formed a beautiful bond with this city.

MEDIA

May 2013—Trade of Innocence

A national Christian bookstore approached us to assist with a strategy to release *Trade of Innocents*, a film dealing with human trafficking.

A team of leaders involved in the area, including a Youth With A Mission missionary who has a ministry outreach to 120 brothels, were brought together and a strategy was formed. Following the screening of the film, key groups were given the platform to speak, and a petition to request a federal anti-trafficking ambassador was created. Again theatres were filled and significant awareness of this critical issue was advanced. The project strongly cemented our relationship with the national bookstore. We now hold our weekly strategic KFC meeting on their premises. The KFC meetings always begin with worship and intimacy with the Lord and waiting on His strategies and blueprints.

August 2012—Understanding of intercession: prayer tower and visit by Apostle Tommi Femrite and Norma Johnson

We were thrilled to receive Apostle Tommi Femrite and Norma Johnson. A meeting was held between intercessors and marketplace businesspeople in one of our largest churches in the city. Another meeting was called, and our boardroom was filled to capacity with the table removed. A strategic prayer assignment was also convened inside the oldest Masonic lodge in Australasia, and valuable intelligence was gathered.

Conclusion

One of the key reasons we attribute these advancements to the existence of the prayer tower in the heart of the city for over twelve years. The cooperation and the culture of honor between the intercessors and marketplace leaders has been a great blessing to this city. We pay special tribute to Jenny and her team. I am in awe at what the Lord has done and am grateful and overjoyed by the apostolic guidance of ambassadors like John Kelly, Chris Peterson, Naomi Dowdy, John Alley, Tommi Femrite, Dexter Low, and Tan Tek Seng.

The KFC standing army is a covenantal company of champions modeling a glimpse of what true unity is and could be. Each member is an inspiration and a joy to me and each other.

We will, by God's grace, continue to call, refresh, introduce, and support the hurting and discouraged champions, and the curse of poverty will be broken. The Father's heart will be reflected in every sphere.

APPENDIX 4
CAN *a* NATION BE TRANSFORMED *in a* DAY?

From Sri Lanka, January 8–9, 2015
Written and Reported by Apostle Woodrow
Blok, Colombo, Sri Lanka

FOR SEVERAL YEARS, groups of senior pastors and leaders of churches and ministries in Sri Lanka have been coming together to pray. Approximately two hundred evangelical leaders from across all denominational lines meet for prayer and also have an annual retreat and a prayer rally. They come together in unity and pray for the Lord to do a mighty work in the nation. According to some journalists, the nation of Sri Lanka has been one of the most corrupt nations in modern history.

A TIME OF GREAT SHAKING BROUGHT ABOUT AN UNBELIEVABLE CHANGE

Answered prayer:

> Who has heard such a thing? Who has seen such things? Shall the earth be made to give birth in one day? Or *shall a nation be born at once?*
> —ISAIAH 66:8, EMPHASIS ADDED

Yes, our nation was reborn on January 8 and 9! It has been amazing to see the answered prayers. The New Year 2015 turned up with a huge clashing bang, thundering, for us here in Sri Lanka.

Sri Lanka has never had a revival in the history of the nation! Join with us in praying for revival. The time is now.

When we returned to Sri Lanka on November 22, 2014, we had been in the United States of America and Canada for seven weeks. The incumbent president of Sri Lanka, Mahinda Rajapaksa, had called a snap poll for a presidential election. The date was set for January 8, 2015! He chose to call the election early even though he had two years more to complete his second term. The ruling officials manipulate and change important national events whenever they choose. It is unpredictable and has the traits of a banana republic, which causes instability in a nation. The nation under Rajapaksa's leadership was heading toward a powerful totalitarian state with China as its role model and mentor. Sri Lanka, since it was granted its independence in 1948, has been—at least on paper—a democratic nation.

However—surprise, surprise! After announcing the poll date for voting, a senior minister and general secretary of his party suddenly without any warning defected to the opposition side and became the most powerful challenger to the presidency. With the help of a former president and an astute opposition leader, he drew many reputable political parties together to present a huge challenge to the incumbent.

The church at large, including our fellowship of churches, called a thirty-three-day prayer watch from December 8, 2014, to January 9, 2015. Hundreds prayed daily for at least an hour for God's chosen person to be appointed. Seventy-two hours of uninterrupted worship and intercession were held from December 31 to January 3, 2015. Powerful! Another 24-hour prayer watch continued on election day, starting January 8 and continuing into the reporting of results the next day. Thousands joined!

Our intercessors had visions of the president's hand turning dark black and withering to the bone. This particular hand had clutched on to a pure gold amulet that has been chanted over by astrologers and witches for 24/7 protection and success at the polls. He carried his amulet everywhere he went, even on his overseas travels. His personal nationally known "Royal Astrologer" predicted publicly that President Rajapaksa would win easily, as January 8 was a very lucky day for him. The astrologer set the date for the elections! This false prophet predicted that it would be easier than the first and second presidential elections held five and ten years earlier.

Two days before the election, I [Woody] was called on to pray at a gathering of Christian ministers convened at a leading senior politician's residence. This man, John Amaratunga, eventually became a minister in the government's cabinet. Mr. Amaratunga, besides holding other portfolios, is also the Minister for Christian Affairs, which is a department that was so very, very, very needed. Now we have a ministry established by the government, and the grievances for severe persecution that the church has faced over the last fifteen years can have a voice. Previously, our grievances would go to the Ministry of Buddhist Affairs, where it was like going from the frying pan to the fire!

While the votes were being counted, it was during the night that the incumbent, Mr. Rajapaksa, realized he was losing the election. He made a valiant attempt to conduct a military coup so he could remain in power for a third term. At about 2:00 a.m. on January 9, we heard about the attempt and pressed through in intercession to block a military takeover. The military had been dispatched all over the city of Colombo and other key locations. However, several key players like the army commander, the attorney general, the elections commissioner, and other influential voices just refused to support him. Praise God! The president finally decided to leave peacefully before daylight and hand over power.

The atmosphere in the nation has made a huge difference! Astrology and witchcraft were publicly defeated and denounced very strongly. Corruption, nepotism, totalitarianism, human rights abuse, and all the rest have been defeated to some degree, at least for now! The spell that hung over the people has been broken. People are starting to feel the freedom once again after many years.

This time the church in Sri Lanka did it right, for which we are very thankful! There was a sovereign work of God taking place. The Lord showed me clearly that the current president would be voted in, but that he wouldn't come in without a huge fight. His coup attempt was expected, but the good news is that the church prayed through and defeated the threat completely! As God's people, we truly can take dominion as the *ecclesia* over the darkness hanging over our nations. We can make a big difference if we get involved. If the coup had been successful, the nation could have been under a dictator for many, many years to come. Even though the horse is prepared for battle, victory does come from the Lord! (Prov. 21:31).

Today, January 19, Melanie [Woody's wife] and I attended a prayer dedication ceremony at the office of recently appointed government minister Rosy Senanayake, a dedicated Christian. This is historic as she is one of two committed Christians in the new government. There are five Christians including Catholics in the new administration. This will give the church a higher degree of favor, more than has been known in the history of the nation.

Our ministry had been meeting, praying, and counseling with Rosy Senanayake for over seven years while she was in the opposition. Only last year she was contemplating giving up politics, but we encouraged her to keep going and not quit! We believed that God had a purpose for calling Rosy into this arena. He would be the One to promote her, and maybe even do it very "suddenly"! That very word materialized one year later. She has been promoted to State Minister of Children's Affairs and is holding a responsible position where Christians are a major minority.

Our nation is blessed because of diligent prayer and the gracious hand of God!

> Ask of Me, and I will give You the nations for Your inheritance, and the ends of the earth for Your possession.
> —PSALM 2:8

We ask for your continued prayer. The official religion in our nation is Buddhism. With a population of 21.6 million, less than 2 percent are evangelical Christians. According to the UK's Open Doors Watch List, which highlights the countries where it is most difficult to live as a Christian, Sri Lanka ranks 44th, and the source of the persecution is religious nationalism and extremism!ꞌ

NOTES

Introduction
God's Mandate for Transforming Your Nation

1. Siegfrid Alegado, "Philippines Holds Benchmark Rate as Asia Braces for Outflows," *Bloomberg Business*, December 17, 2015, http://www.bloomberg.com/news/articles/2015-12-17/philippines-holds-benchmark-rate-as-asia-braces-for-outflows.

2. The Heritage Foundation, 2015 Index of Economic Freedom, accessed February 16, 2016, http://www.heritage.org/index/pdf/2015/countries/philippines.pdf.

Chapter 1
Make Disciples of All Nations

1. Ralph D. Winters, *Perspectives on the World Christian Movement* (Pasadena, CA: William Carey Library, 1981), 312–313.

2. C. Peter Wagner, *The Church in the Workplace* (Ventura, CA: Regal Books, 2006), 114.

3. Tabitha Rani and Kim Teoh, "The Enterprising Pastor," *Asian Beacon*, August 18, 2013, accessed February 10, 2016, http://asianbeacon.org/the-enterprising-pastor/.

4. Ibid.

5. Ibid.

6. Wagner, *The Church in the Workplace*, 41–42.

7. 2006 World Population Data Sheet, Population Reference Bureau, accessed February 10, 2016, http://www.prb.org/pdf06/06worlddatasheet.pdf.

8. Philippines Poverty Assessment, Volume 1: Main Report, The World Bank, Poverty Reduction and Economic Management Unit, East Asia and Pacific Region, May 31, 2001, http://www-wds.worldbank.org/servlet/WDSContentServer/WDSP/IB/2002/01/07/000094946_01121904064580/Rendered/PDF/multipage.pdf. See also the Philippines Statistics Authority poverty statistics, http://www.nscb.gov.ph/poverty/; http://www.indexmundi.com/g/r.aspx?c=rp&v=69.

Chapter 2
Thy Kingdom Come

1. George Eldon Ladd, *The Gospel of the Kingdom* (Grand Rapids, MI: Wm. B. Eerdmans Publishing Company, 1981), 21.

Chapter 3
Dealing with Mind-Sets

1. "Jefferson's Wall of Separation Letter," US Constitution Online, http://www.usconstitution.net/jeffwall.html.

2. The exact scope of the Western world is somewhat subjective in nature, depending on whether cultural, economic, spiritual or political criteria are employed. But these definitions almost always include the countries of Western

Europe, North America, Israel, Australia, and New Zealand. These are Western European or Western European-derived nations that enjoy relatively strong econo-mies and stable governments, allow freedom of religion, have chosen democracy as a form of governance, favor capitalism and international trade, are heavily influ-enced by Judeo-Christian values, and have some form of political and military alli-ance or cooperation. (Wikipedia.org, s.v. "Western World," accessed February 11, 2016, http://en.wikipedia.org/wiki/Western_world.)

3. Encyclopedia Britannica Online, s.v. "Charlemagne," July 11, 2007, http://www.britannica.com/biography/Charlemagne. In AD 800, Pope Leo III ordained Charlemagne as Imperator Romanorum, literally "Emperor of the Romans," a title reserved for the emperor of the Western Roman Empire. Charlemagne had ear-lier supported the pope against the Romans who were seeking to depose the pope. Nevertheless, the new crown and title would have given Charlemagne a greater prestige and influence over his empire, which spanned Western Europe.

4. "During the Middle Ages and in Renaissance times, the Swiss had the repu-tation of being among Europe's best and most reliable mercenary soldiers, meaning they fought well and did not change sides in mid-battle, as was wont to happen from time to time. The pope's private army was set up in Rome in 1506 and many members of the Swiss Guard gave their lives protecting the pope during the sack of Rome a few years later... The conditions of recruitment are severe—candidates have to be practicing Catholics, to have completed their compulsory military ser-vice in Switzerland and to be of irreproachable character." (David Willey, "First Non-White Joins Vatican Guard," BBC News, July 4, 2002, accessed September 3, 2007, http://news.bbc.co.uk/1/hi/world/europe/2092406.stm.)

5. Frederick the Wise, as he was known, was Luther's prince, and was instru-mental in orchestrating a "kidnapping" to protect Luther's life after the imperial Edict of Worms of 1521 which essentially made it lawful for anyone to kill him. Encyclopedia Britannica Online, s.v. "Frederick III," July 14, 2007, http://www.britannica.com/biography/Frederick-III-elector-of-Saxony.

6. See http://www.pilgrimhall.org/PSNoteNewReligiousControversies.htm. Website owned and operated by the Pilgrim Society, which was incorporated by the General Court of the Commonwealth of Massachusetts in 1820 to memorialize the history of the Pilgrims. (Not to be confused with the Pilgrims Society.)

7. Hope Taylor's message at the Latter Rain Church National Convention, 2006. Hope serves as Director of the International Leadership Embassy in Wash-ington DC. He is the Apostolic Leader of Church of the King in La Grange, Georgia. You can read more about Hope's ministry at http://www.ile-dc.org.

8. Francis Frangipane, *Repairers of the Breach* (Cedar Rapids, IA., Arrow Pub-lications, 1994), 17.

9. Wagner, *The Church in the Workplace*, 53.

10. Sarah Eekhof Zylstra, "Small Loans, Big Goals," *Christianity Today* 50, no. 12 (December 2006): 14, http://www.christianitytoday.com/ct/2006/december/3.14.html.

11. Kenneth Scott Latourette, *A History of Christianity* (New York: Harper & Row, 1975), 429.

12. Rene Q. Bas, under the "Catholic Church" column, *The Manila Times*, July 2, 2008, A5.

13. Ibid.

14. Wagner, *The Church in the Workplace*, 56–57.

Chapter 4
Influencing the Molders of Culture

1. Wagner, *The Church in the Workplace*, 113–115.

2. The World Factbook, Central Intelligence Agency, Washington DC, 2013–2014, accessed February 16, 2016, https://www.cia.gov/library/publications/the-world-factbook/fields/2122.html.

3. Ibid.

4. "Malaysia Population," Trading Economics, accessed February 8, 2014, http://www.tradingeconomics.com/malaysia/population.

5. Solomon Bulan and Lillian Bulan-Dorai, *The Bario Revival* (Kuala Lumpur, Malaysia: Home Matters Network, 2004), 17.

6. "World Teleport Association Picks for Top Seven Intelligent Communities in the World," World Teleport Association, accessed February 13, 2016, http://www.unimas.my/ebario/award2.htm.

7. Bulan and Bulan-Dorai, *The Bario Revival*, 208.

8. Accessed February 8, 2014, http://www.mountmurud.com/pdf/PDF-%20Ba-Kelalan-Miracles.pdf.

9. Melanie M. Reyes, "Migration and Filipino Children Left-Behind: A Literature Review," United Nations Children's Fund, accessed February 8, 2014, http://www.unicef.org/philippines/Synthesis_StudyJuly12008.pdf.

10. James C. McKinley Jr., "Texas Conservatives Win Curriculum Changes," *The New York Times*, March 12, 2010, http://www.nytimes.com/2010/03/13/education/13texas.html?_r=0.

11. "Texas Gives the Boot to Liberal Social Studies Bias," America's Party News, April 27, 2010, accessed February 8, 2014, http://www.aipnews.com/talk/forums/thread-view.asp?tid=13700&posts=1.

12. Lauren Carroll, "Under Common Core, Teaching Simple Addition Takes a Full Minute, Texas Governor Says," Politifact, February 3, 2015, accessed February 16, 2016, http://www.politifact.com/truth-o-meter/statements/2015/feb/03/greg-abbott/under-common-core-teaching-simple-addition-takes-f/.

13. Wikipedia, s.v. "Facing the Giants," accessed February 16, 2016, https://en.wikipedia.org/wiki/Facing_the_Giants.

14. Wikipedia, s.v. "Fireproof (film)," accessed February 16, 2016, https://en.wikipedia.org/wiki/Fireproof_(film).

Chapter 5
Spiritual Warfare: Keys to Transforming a Nation

1. C. Peter Wagner, *Praying with Power* (Shippensburg, PA: Destiny Image Publishers, Inc., 1997), 84.

2. The term *third world* was originally coined in times of the Cold War to distinguish those nations that are neither aligned with the West (NATO) nor with the East, the Communist bloc. Today the term is often used to describe the developing countries of Africa, Asia, Latin America, and Oceania. Many poorer nations adopted the term to describe themselves.

3. Cindy Jacobs told me this personally and also mentioned it during her class on Spiritual Warfare under the section, "Remitting Sins of the Nations," in the School of World Mission, Fuller Theological Seminary, one of the Advanced Church Growth classes under Professor C. Peter Wagner.

4. Dr. Paul Ariga, chair of Japan Church Growth Institute Networks, also serves as president of the All Japan Revival Mission.

5. Santiago Padua, "Argentina's Stock Market Is All About US Dollars," CFA Institute, November 25, 2013, https://blogs.cfainstitute.org/investor/2013/11/25 /argentinas-stock-market-is-all-about-us-dollars/.

6. "IMF Executive Board Concludes the 2006 Article IV Consultation with the Philippines," International Monetary Fund, Public Information Notice No. 07/14, February 7, 2007, http://www.imf.org/external/np/sec/pn/2007/pn0714.htm.

7. Philip Gerson, "Poverty and Economic Policy in the Philippines," International Monetary Fund, *Finance & Development* 35, no. 3 (September 1998): n.p., http://www.imf.org/external/pubs/ft/fandd/1998/09/gerson.htm.

8. Allana Welch, "Latest Statistics on Philippine Poverty," The Borgen Project, July 11, 2013, http://borgenproject.org/latest-statistics-on-philippine-poverty/.

Chapter 6
Linking Generations

1. Craig von Buseck, "George Otis, Sr.: Another Christian General Goes Home," CBN, July 24, 2007, accessed February 13, 2016, http://www1.cbn.com /ChurchWatch/archive/2007/08/16/george-otis-sr.-another-christian-general-goes -home.

2. Wikipedia, s.v. "YTL Corporation," accessed February 13, 2016, http:// en.wikipedia.org/wiki/YTL_Corporation.

3. Ibid.

4. YTL Community News, April 9, 2009. See also Tony Hii, "Tan Sri Dato' Francis Yeoh's Sharing," Tonyhii.com, May 3, 2009, Blog entry, http://wwwtonyhii .blogspot.com/2009/05/tan-sri-dato-francis-yeohs-sharing.html.

5. Low Yit Leng, "Creating Magical Moment," *Prestige* Magazine, May 2010, http://www.ytlcommunity.com/commnews/shownews.asp?newsid=53298.

6. David Demian, *The Kingdom Experiment* (magazine published for the Watchmen for the Nations), 2012, 7; accessed February 13, 2016, http://www .asiagathering.hk/wp-content/uploads/2012/TKE_Eng.pdf.

7. Ibid.

8. T. W. Farnam, "Obama Has Aggressive Internet Strategy to Woo Supporters," *The Washington Post*, April 6, 2012, https://www.washingtonpost.com /politics/obama-has-aggressive-internet-strategy-to-woo-supporters/2012/04/06 /gIQAavB2zS_story.html; Michael Scherer, "Friended: How the Obama Campaign Connected with Young Voters," *Time*, November 20, 2012, http:// swampland.time.com/2012/11/20/friended-how-the-obama-campaign-connected -with-young-voters/.

9. Michael Scherer, "Exclusive: Obama's 2012 Digital Fundraising Outperformed 2008," *Time*, November 15, 2012, http://swampland.time.com/2012/11/15 /exclusive-obamas-2012-digital-fundraising-outperformed-2008/; "Obama Sets All-Time Fundraising Record, Crushes Final Romney Totals," CBS DC, December 7, 2012, http://washington.cbslocal.com/2012/12/07/obama-sets-all-time-fundraising -record-crushed-final-romney-totals/.

10. James Poniewozik, "Iranians Protest Election, Tweeps Protest CNN," Tuned In Blog, *Time*, June 15, 2009, http://tunedin.blogs.time.com/2009/06/15 /iranians-protest-election-tweeps-protest-cnn; see also Simon Robinson, "Was Ahmadinejad's Win Rigged?" *Time*, June 15, 2009, http://content.time.com/time /specials/packages/article/0,28804,1904645_1904644,00.html.

Chapter 7
Touching Heaven, Changing Earth

1. Jim Hodges, *What in the World Is the Church to Do? The Seven Corporate Ministries of the Church* (Duncanville, TX: Federation of Ministers and Churches International), 29.

Chapter 8
The Action Plan for Nation Transformation

1. Wikipedia, s.v. "William Wilberforce," accessed February 13, 2016, http:// en.wikipedia.org/wikiWilliam Wilberforce.

2. For more information, visit http://www.ile-dc.org/.

3. For more information, visit http://www.icaleaders.com/nations/.

4. Taken from the Watchmen for the Nations website, accessed December 12, 2006, http://www.watchmen.org/Journey/index.asp.

5. Ibid; see also Jeff King, "Let Us Weep for Zion," *Charisma News*, July 31, 2001, http://www.charismanews.com/opinion/standing-with-israel/47797-let-us -weep-for-zion.

6. "Fourth Election in Seven Years Expands Conservative Party's Hold," Infoplease.com, accessed February 14, 2016, http://www.infoplease.com/ipa /A0107386.html?pageno=8.

7. "2006 World Population Data Sheet," Population Reference Bureau, accessed February 15, 2016, http://www.prb.org/pdf06/06worlddatasheet.pdf. The poverty line is defined here as "the percentage of the population with average consumption expenditures less than $2.15 per day measured in 1993 prices converted using

purchasing power parity (PPP) rates. The World Bank's estimates are drawn from surveys that use common methods for measuring household living standards across countries."

8. "Poverty Incidence among Filipinos Registered at 25.8 Percent, as of First Semester of 2014–PSA," Republic of the Philippines Philippine Statistics Authority, March 6, 2015, http://nap.psa.gov.ph/poverty/default.asp.

Chapter 9
Convergence

1. Cindy Jacobs, *The Reformation Manifesto* (Minneapolis, MN: Bethany House Publishers, 2008), 14.

2. Ibid., 18.

3. John Benefiel, *Binding the Strongman over America: Healing the Land, Transferring Wealth, Advancing the Kingdom of God* (Oklahoma City, OK: Benefiel Ministries, Inc., 2012), Introduction.

4. Ibid., 27.

5. Ibid.

6. Ibid.

7. Ibid., 29.

8. Ibid., 32.

9. Ibid., 220; for further documented information, see Ibid., 220–221.

10. Information in this list is based on the Session done by Kathleen Liska, HAPN State Co-Leader for Alaska, on November 1, 2014.

11. Native American Apology Resolution (2009), 111th Congress, 1st Session, S. J. Res. 14. Library of Congress. http://thomas.loc.gov/cgi-bin/query/z?c111:S.J.RES.14 .IS; see also Benefiel, *Binding the Strongman*, 145.

12. For more information, visit www.asiagathering.hk or contact them at inquiry@asiagathering.hk.

13. Mariko Kato, "Christianity's Long History in the Margins," *The Japan Times*, February 24, 2009, http://www.japantimes.co.jp/news/2009/02/24/reference /christianitys-long-history-in-the-margins/#.VtXZoOmoPIV.

14. Demian, *The Kingdom Experiment*, 6.

15. Ibid., 5.

16. Ibid., 7.

17. Ibid.

18. Ibid., 10.

19. Ibid., 13.

20. Ibid.

21. Ibid.

22. Ibid.

23. Ibid.

24. Ibid., 15.

25. Ibid., 18.

26. Ibid., 19.

27. Ibid., 20.

28. Wikipedia, s.v. "Economy of the Philippines," accessed February 12, 2016, https://en.wikipedia.org/wiki/Economy_of_the_Philippines.

29. Clarissa Batino, Ditas Lopez, and Cecilia Yap, "Pope's Defense of Poor Shows Challenge for Philippines," Bloomberg, January 19, 2015, http://www .bloomberg.com/news/articles/2015-01-19/pope-francis-defense-of-the-poor-shows -challenge-for-philippines.

30. Richard Javad Heydarian, "The Philippines: The Next Asian Tiger economy?," *Al Jazeera*, June 14, 2014, http://www.aljazeera.com/indepth /opinion/2014/06/philippines-asian-tiger-econom-2014612144132483842.html.

31. Alberto Leandro Llaryora, "Rise and Shine with the Philippines," *Our World*, supplement to *USA TODAY*, June 17, 2013, 1, http://www.theworldfolio.com/files /old/1370854755.pdf.

32. Deputy Governor Diwa Guinigundo, "Credit Surety Fund: Empowering MSME through Access to Bank Credit," *Manila Bulletin*, July 3, 2014, SS–2.

33. Ibid.

34. Daron Acemoglu and James A. Robinson, *Why Nations Fail: The Origins of Power, Prosperity, and Poverty* (New York: Crown Publishers, 2012), 454.

35. Ibid., 81.

Conclusion
Where Do We Go From Here?

1. David Cannistraci, *The Gift of Apostle* (Ventura, CA: Regal Books, 1996), 85.

2. Mark W. Pfeifer, *Alignment* (Chillicothe, OH: SOMA Family of Ministries, 2008), 195.

3. Ibid., 197.

4. See http://www.economist.com/media/pdf/QUALITY_OF_LIFE.pdf.

Appendix 1
Nations

1. *Enciclopedia Italiana Vol. 1*, "The Voyages of Pedro de Quiros," 1949, 163–5; see also Sze Leng Chan, "Celebration of the Prophetic Declaration for Australia," Christian Today, May 10, 2006, accessed March 31, 2016, http://www .christiantoday.com.au/article/celebration.of.the.prophetic.declaration.for .australia/2324.htm.

2. Tom Phillips, "China on Course to Become 'World's Most Christian Nation' Within 15 Years," *The Telegraph*, April 19, 2014, http://www.telegraph.co.uk/news /worldnews/asia/china/10776023/China-on-course-to-become-worlds-most -Christian-nation-within-15-years.html; see also http://www.billionbibles.org/china /how-many-christians-in-china.html.

Appendix 2
Taking the Kingdom of God into the Marketplace

1. Diagram created by Peter Kentley.

Appendix 3
Report to the International Coalition of Apostles

1. Julie Peterson, "'Suing the Devil' Ranks in Top 12 Films on Walmart's On Demand," Christian News Wire, April 18, 2012, accessed April 21, 2016, http://www.christiannewswire.com/news/9216019469.html.

Appendix 4
Can a Nation be Transformed in a Day?

1. The Open Doors Report 2015, "Freedom of Religion and the Persecution of Christians," https://www.opendoorsuk.org/advocacy/documents/world_watch _report.pdf.

ABOUT *the* AUTHOR

$\mathcal{D}$EXTER AND HIS wife, Lily Low, are the founders of the Latter Rain Church of Malaysia, an indigenous apostolic church movement with churches throughout the nation. Over the years, they have mentored and raised many leaders and workers as they ministered in many nations. Apostolic and prophetic ministers, they operate in the power of the Holy Spirit with a strong prophetic anointing and impart, activate, and empower those they train.

Dexter was the coordinator of Southeast Asia's Spiritual Warfare Network (AD2000 Movement) and a member of the Apostolic Roundtable under the leadership of Dr. C. Peter Wagner. He also serves as vice-president of the Asia for Christ Movement, and he and Lily are members of the Australian Coalition of Apostolic Leaders. Dexter is a member of Global Spheres and International Coalition of Apostolic Leaders. Both Dexter and Lily are active in the FMCI (Federation of Ministries and Churches) based in Dallas, Texas, under the leadership of Jim Hodges, and International Breakthrough Ministries of Barbara Wentroble. They are actively involved with Apostle John Benefiel in the HAPN (Heartland Apostolic Prayer Network) based in Oklahoma City.

Dexter holds a Licentiate of Theology (LTh) from Melbourne College of Divinity, a Diploma of Theology (DipTh) from Singapore, a Bachelor of Divinity (BD) from England, a Master of Arts in Missiology (MA) from Fuller Theological Seminary, a Doctor of Practical Ministry (DPMin) from Wagner Leadership Institute, and Doctor of Theology (ThD) from Promise Christian University based in California.

Dexter's burden is to see the church play its rightful role as an agency for social transformation of communities, cities, and nations.

In the Philippines Dexter was a prime mover, and he and Lily together were speakers in both Touching Heaven, Changing Earth I (May 2005) and II (March 2007). Dexter spoke at the recent conference in Dipolog City, September 2014. Touching Heaven, Changing Earth conferences are organized by BSP (Bangko Sentral ng Pilipinas, or the Philippines Central Bank, which is equivalent to the Federal Reserve) Christian Fellowship, which is fast becoming a national movement for the transformation of the nation of the Philippines. To date, this movement for the transformation of the Philippines has conducted conferences in thirty-seven cities.

His ministry has extended to Australia and Sri Lanka besides Southeast Asia.

In Malaysia he is currently involved in the Fathers of the Nation Gathering, bringing spiritual fathers of the nation together regionally and nationally to pray for the nation. He is also a council member of NECF (National Evangelical Christian Fellowship) of Malaysia.

Currently, Dexter and Lily Low serve as senior pastors of the Latter Rain Church, basing themselves at Vision Valley Center in Petaling Jaya (Selangor, Malaysia). They have five children and ten grandchildren (so far).

CONTACT *the* AUTHOR

To contact Dr. Low through the mail, write to:

340 S. Lemon Ave. #3388
Walnut, CA 91789
United States